The Art of Conversation

The Art of Conversation

DIALOGUE AT THE WOODROW WILSON CENTER

George Liston Seay

Edited by Peter J. Bean

WOODROW WILSON CENTER PRESS · WASHINGTON, DC
THE JOHNS HOPKINS UNIVERSITY PRESS · BALTIMORE, MD

EDITORIAL OFFICES
Woodrow Wilson Center Press
Woodrow Wilson International Center for Scholars
One Woodrow Wilson Plaza
1300 Pennsylvania Avenue, N.W.
Washington, D.C. 20004-3027
Telephone: 202-691-4010
www.wilsoncenter.org

ORDER FROM
The Johns Hopkins University Press
Hampden Station
P.O. Box 50370
Baltimore, Maryland 21211
Telephone: 1-800-537-5487
www.press.jhu.edu/books

The poetry in chapter 22 is used with the permission of Deborah Darr.

2 4 6 8 9 7 5 3 1

Library of Congress Cataloging-in-Publication Data

Seay, George Liston.
  The art of conversation : Dialogue at the Woodrow Wilson Center / George
Liston Seay ; edited by Peter J. Bean
    p. cm.
  ISBN 978-0-8018-8783-3 (cloth : alk. paper)
  1. United States—Foreign relations—1989—Miscellanea. 2. World politics—
1989—Miscellanea. 3. United States—Intellectual life—Miscellanea. 4.
Intellectual life—Miscellanea. 5. Conversation—Miscellanea. 6. Politicians—
Interviews. 7. Intellectuals—Interviews. 8. Authors—Interviews. 9. Interviews—
Washington (D.C.) I. Bean, Peter J. II. Dialogue (Radio program) III. Title.
  E840.S394   2007
  973.928—dc22

                                                              2007045702

CONTENTS

Part II: American Leaders, Prophets, and Critics

Part III: Thinkers, Poets, and Playwrights

PREFACE

✺

In September of 1988, the late Charles Blitzer, then director of the Woodrow Wilson International Center for Scholars, came to me with an invitation: Would I like to revive the Center's radio programs, which had aired from 1983 to 1987? Sensing an adventure, I answered with an enthusiastic yes, and followed with a question of my own: How much time would I have for training and practice before my first broadcast? Looking pained, Charles told me that he hoped we could be on the air in two weeks.

And we were. *dialogue* was launched, on schedule, in October of 1988, and the pace has not slackened from that time to this.

Nearly twenty years and nine hundred programs later, a great deal has changed since that first hectic broadcast (whose subject was, perhaps suitably, chaos theory). We have achieved world-wide distribution for a program that is now produced in our own studio, and we have added television to our weekly schedule. *dialogue* has won a number of awards, and some thirty-eight programs have been placed in the permanent collection of the Museum of Television and Radio. I am especially proud that *dialogue* is archived in the libraries of forty-two American colleges and universities.

What impresses me most, though, is what remains unchanged. *dialogue* is still a place where ideas are central and where, I hope, our guests' passion for ideas comes through. For that reason,

although I have always cringed at any reference to *dialogue* as a "talk show," I have never hesitated to describe it as an ongoing conversation about ideas.

That brings me to the title we chose for this collection. I wasn't long into hosting the program before I learned that conversation is an art, and not a minor one at that. Real conversation, which I take to be the mutual exploration of a significant subject, is fundamental to our sense of ourselves as reasoning social beings. Chat, gossip, small-talk, and banter may get us through the day, but only when we seriously converse do we find real connections and forge greater understanding. That marvelous phrase of C.S. Lewis's, "the joy of people who take each other seriously," sums it up perfectly.

And the phrase may also suggest why *dialogue* is such an appropriate part of the Woodrow Wilson Center. Through *dialogue* the immediacy of the image and the impact of the spoken word spreads beyond our walls in a way that complements the Center's print and website offerings. Our broadcasts accentuate the essential human dimension of the Center's public mission and, we hope, make possible an expanded conversation about ideas.

Most important, *dialogue* reflects the Center's spirit. Our programs are not built upon celebrity and controversy, but rather upon content and candor. The twenty-four programs presented here represent the breadth of a series that covers the intellectual waterfront from poetry to politics, history to heroism. While many of our guests are well known, others are not. They are not necessarily people you have heard of, but they are people you should hear from.

ACKNOWLEDGMENTS

The work that brings *dialogue* forth is done by a small but extraordinary team of people. Over the years that team has changed but, without exception, the excellence and collegiality that distinguish *dialogue's* staff remain constant. The names of all *dialogue* staff, past and present, appear at the end of this book.

I must make special mention of our producer John Tyler and associate producer Shaarona Harris. Together, they did so much to make this book possible. In this they joined Peter Bean, whose talented editing caught the essence of the conversations and the spirit of our program. Trips down memory lane with Peter were a special delight for me.

Equally brilliant and indispensable to this project were the contributions of our publisher Joe Brinley and his staff Yamile Kahn and Erin Mosely, editor Robert Landers, designer Debra Naylor, and illustrator Talia Greenberg. And like all of us here at the Center, I am indebted to Lee Hamilton and Mike Van Dusen for a style of leadership whose hallmark is support and encouragement. They, and my other Center colleagues, created an atmosphere that made work on this book a constant joy.

PART I

The United States
and the World

1

Lee H. Hamilton

U.S. Foreign Policy in a Changing World

What's remarkable about a conversation with Lee Hamilton is how easy it is. Down to earth and direct in his style, Lee's authenticity underscores everything he says and makes him a force for practical politics. As a leader of two bipartisan, high-powered bodies studying divisive problems—vice-chair of the 9/11 Commission and co-chair of the Iraq Study Group—he was key to forging sets of recommendations that were not only bold but also unanimous. Lee served in Congress from 1965 to 1999 as a representative from Indiana. He has been president and director of the Woodrow Wilson Center since 1999.

George Seay: Lee, you served in Congress for thirty-four years, you worked with seven Presidents, eleven Secretaries of State, and during all that time focused on foreign policy, so it's safe to say that you are an expert on this topic.

In 1965, the year you entered Congress, the dominant issues were the Cold War and Vietnam. What does the situation look like to a freshman Congressman today?

Hamilton: It's a very different world. When I came into the Congress, the single foreign policy issue really was Vietnam. The whole country was focused on Vietnam and that was true for the first two or three years of my Congressional career.

Today's world is in many ways a more complex world, and terrorism is the great concern at the moment. It's a more uncertain world. It's a world that's more dangerous to the American people because for the first time we've learned that we're not safe in our communities and in our homes. Today's members of Congress face a different kind of war than the more traditional war of Vietnam.

GS: On the other side, do you at the same time see opportunities for a country like ours, a country that's the only superpower in this world?

Hamilton: Certainly, we often focus on the problems, as your question suggested, but we also have enormous opportunities. As a matter of fact, I don't know of any time in American history when we've had the kind of opportunities that we have today to shape the world we live in. America is the largest and strongest power—not just here, but anywhere on the face of the globe. We have unprecedented military, economic, cultural, soft, and hard power, and that provides us with enormous opportunities to make the world better.

GS: Another thing that strikes me, when I think of those in Congress today, is that there has been a great increase in the number of people trying to influence American foreign policy. Can you give us a sense of how that changes the process?

Hamilton: Some years ago, the only players were the president, a few leaders of the Congress, the president of the World Bank, and the secretary general of the United Nations.

Today you can make a long list of players who impact American foreign policy, and many of them are nongovernmental. That makes it more difficult to form a consensus. And keep in mind that the American government, whether you're talking about domestic or international matters, doesn't function very well unless you've got a consensus.

GS: One of the actors that seems to be especially important is the media.

Hamilton: There's no doubt that the media are enormously important—particularly, I think, as agenda setters. If the cameras are rolling in Somalia and you're showing starving children with distended bellies, the American people sitting at home will say to themselves, "We can't tolerate that. We should try to help."

Now, when those cameras shift and begin to show American Marines being shot up in Somalia, that too impacts the American people and they say, "We can't stand that. We need to bring those troops out of there."

The media were not present in Rwanda, for example, when there was a genocide taking place, so the United States turned its head. The media, along with the president, are the principal agenda-setters for American foreign policy.

The president is the only person in the American political system who has the attention of all the American people. He has all kinds of responsibilities, but one of his most important ones is to explain the world in which we live, its challenges, its opportunities, its problems, and the American role in dealing with those problems.

One of the things I often tried to do was to get presidents to articulate policy. Presidents don't like to do it because it's so difficult. It's hard to get a consensus within the executive branch. Every word they say is broadcast all over the world. There are a lot of audiences out there. It's a very tough thing to do, but it's terribly important that the American people know, that Congress know, and that the president's cabinet know what his policies are. And in order to do that, a president must speak frequently, articulately, clearly, and precisely about America's role in the world, his vision of America's role, and what he's prepared to do to try to achieve that.

GS: What is Congress's role in foreign policy today?

Hamilton: Congress today is very diffuse—the power is separated. The days are gone when the president could call up someone like Senator Arthur Vandenberg or Senator Lyndon Johnson, and ask what the feeling in the Senate or the House was. Power is much more dispersed, so Congress has some real handicaps in its foreign policy role.

Congress has to be both critic and partner. It has to be a critic in telling a president when he's off base and suggest certain modifications, but overall the Congress should try to be constructive and supportive of American foreign policy.

I happen to think that Congress brings some strengths to the process of developing American foreign policy that a president does not have, because it is the most representative branch of government. If you want to criticize American foreign policy, you can't call up the president and say, "Mr. President, I'd like to chat with you for a few minutes about your foreign policy." You can't call up the secretary of state or the assistant secretary of state. You can call up a member of Congress or your senator and have your views known. Congress is accessible and much more representative of the American people than the executive branch. These strengths Congress brings to the process are very important.

GS: In 1973, when you were in Congress, the War Powers Act was passed, which clearly reflected concerns over the way the Gulf of Tonkin resolution had been passed. The question of what to do in Iraq is very much before the country right now. What's your sense of how the War Powers Act has worked over the last thirty years and its role in the current situation?

Hamilton: I don't think it's worked very well because it's too complicated. Presidents have never recognized the complexity of it. It binds the president too much. But having said that, the premise of the War Powers Act is a good one. The greatest decision that a country makes is whether or not to send young men and women into war, and that decision should be shared. It should not be made by one person—even the president of the United States. It should be made by both the Congress and the president. I think the Founding Fathers believed that the Congress should commit the country to war, and the president should wage the war.

Now, history moves on and things become more complicated. In the current situation, Congress has really ceded to the president the war-making power. The Iraqi resolution said, in effect, "Mr. President, it's all yours. You make the decision." I'm simplifying here, but that flies in the face of the Constitution and the provision that states that Congress shall declare war. There are many historical reasons for that, but it's where we are.

Having said all of that, I still think that our country should, as much as possible, make the decision to go to war on the basis of a shared decision between the president and the Congress.

GS: Let's use the North American Free Trade Agreement as a test case for this idea of sharing decisions. Our country has had a decade of experience with NAFTA, and I think there is a very strong mood in Washington to seek to extend that free trade throughout the rest of the hemisphere. You and I both know that idea is a subject of some concern and controversy the farther south you go. For example, the recent Brazilian election of a socialist seems to suggest that there is some dubiousness on the part of Brazilians and their president. Now, projecting forward to something that hasn't happened yet, how would Congress and the president best go about working together to try to achieve hemispheric unity, or at least discussion, on this very important trade question?

Hamilton: You're talking about globalization and this remarkable flow of money and people across borders that has come from the revolution in communications and transportation. The Congress and president are not going to turn back globalization. The country and the world benefit from it.

But what we've learned from that Brazilian election and a lot of other places is that globalization is not global. It doesn't help everybody and we have to be much more sensitive to the people left behind, and I think that's where the Congress and the president have to act. You want to extend free trade and you don't want to try to stop the revolution in communications and transportation, or the flow of money across borders. That's all beneficial. But it has to be done in such a way that we are sensitive to the least and the lost of this world.

There are a lot of danger signals that we better pay attention to. The Brazilian election is one, but it's not the only one. People are saying, "You're not paying enough attention to us. You're hogging too much of the world's wealth. You ought to share it more." And anybody who looks at the distribution statistics—not just in Brazil, but in all of Latin America and more and more in the United States—has to be concerned about the distribution of wealth.

It's an enormously difficult problem. You don't want socialism, but nonetheless it's a problem we have to be sensitive to and seek answers for.

GS: How important is dealing with international organizations in accomplishing all this? The United Nations immediately comes to mind, but there are many others. And when we think of our foreign policy interests and bridging these goals that you've spoken of, how important are they to American foreign policy?

Hamilton: First of all, I think America can never cede to the United Nations its sovereign right to make decisions to protect its own national interests. Secondly, I think that we often have to find ways and means of making governance more effective worldwide. I don't have any quick answers for that, but as the world becomes more integrated in an economic sense, we at least have to find mechanisms that let us govern all of these interactions that take place. You don't want an airplane that's taking off from Washington and going to Paris to have no coordination between the air traffic controllers in the two cities. You have to have cooperation, so multilateral institutions are enormously important. I know in the United States there's a certain reluctance about international regimes, but they do far more than most of us recognize, and we need them. To deal with the problem, we have to set them in the context of sovereign nations cooperating with one another.

GS: The tenor of much of what you've been saying about the conduct of foreign policy in this era suggests that new ways of relating, new types of knowledge, and new ways of approaching problems may be really big on the agenda through this decade.

Hamilton: I think the American people do not realize, for example, the extent to which the United Nations has now become the agency that bestows legitimacy. Not for us, particularly—as Americans—but worldwide it has become an extremely important institution.

For example, on the question of intervention, talk to almost anybody who is not an American and they would say that military intervention ought not occur unless it has Security Council approval. That's been one of the debates in New York on the Iraqi resolution. While Americans, for the most part, would not agree with that, it does show you the direction most of the world is going.

There's another dimension to all of this. We're living in a world today where there's a lot of resentment against America, and it's building. It's of two kinds. There is a resentment that is violent. People who hate us and want to kill you and me, and all of our fellow Americans. That's very hard for Americans to understand because we think we're a pretty decent bunch of people, and I think that we are. But those people are out there—we saw their activities on September 11th and in other periods, and we have to respond to that vigorously and robustly.

The other type of resentment is less hostile, but exists none-theless, and you see it in all kinds of places. We saw it in the German election when the chancellor said, "I reject the American approach. I'm not going to send German soldiers into Iraq." You see it in Brazil, when there is an anti-American sentiment that helps elect a president from the populist side of the spectrum.

GS: This second kind of resentment may be maturation. These countries are coming into their own and we have to start recognizing them.

Hamilton: That's particularly true in Europe, where for many years Europe more or less okayed whatever the United States did and worked very closely with us. Today, there are all kinds of strains and stresses in the trans-Atlantic relationship that we've got to begin to deal with. Europe is beginning to feel its oats: it's as large as we are, its economic base is as large as the U.S. base, it's becoming more united, and it is maturing.

GS: You've often spoken about the need to form a "constituency of the whole"—something that brings us all together in terms of a vision. You've also recommended there be something called a "Permanent Foreign Policy Group" created within the Congress to help advise the president. What's the importance of both of those ideas and why would they make things better?

Hamilton: You need a consultative mechanism in Congress that operates on a regular, sustained basis. Sporadic consultation is not enough. And what I'm suggesting is you need to set up a committee of the Congress composed of senior members of the key committees—Republican and Democrat—that would meet regularly with the secretary of state, secretary of defense, the president, and others, to constantly consult on American foreign policy problems and try to broaden the consensus and deal with a lot of problems before they erupt. It's best to deal with problems and try to prevent conflict rather than to react to it.

Originally broadcast October 6, 2004.

2

Robert S. McNamara

The Moral Imperative to Learn from Our Mistakes

Robert S. McNamara was secretary of defense in the Kennedy and Johnson administrations during the buildup of the Vietnam War, the Cuban missile crisis, a refinement of nuclear strategy, and an overhaul of Defense Department planning. Later he became president of the World Bank. Our conversation was one of the most moving experiences I have had at dialogue, for he critically reevaluated his career and seemed to see his lessons as his legacy for others. He was in tears as the conversation ended.

※

George Seay: Robert, you point out that in the twentieth century, 160 million people were slaughtered in warfare—most of them civilians. In this book of yours, *Wilson's Ghost*, you challenge us based on that very statistic to begin to think about American foreign policy on the basis of a moral imperative to make sure that doesn't happen again.[1]

McNamara: Exactly. Is that what we human beings want in the twenty-first century? A repetition of that carnage? I don't, and I

---

1. Robert S. McNamara and James G. Blight, *Wilson's Ghost: Reducing the Risk of Conflict, Killing, and Catastrophe in the 21st Century* (Public Affairs, 2001).

don't think you do, and I don't think your audience does. If we don't, how are we going to avoid it? That's the question this book poses.

GS: And of those 160 million dead, 62 percent were civilians.

McNamara: Men, women, and children. Let me just stop on that one second. On one occasion in March of 1945 I was on the island of Guam as part of the Twentieth Air Force. In a single night, we fire-bombed Tokyo and burned to death 80,000 civilians. Thank God there were reasons for it. We were trying to prevent an invasion. We might have lost a million or so, but these are horrible things and we human beings ought to think about them. We ought to try to avoid them in the future.

GS: Unlike any other book written about foreign policy that I can think of in the recent past, this poses a challenge to Americans and to humanity. You're calling for a radical redefinition of our whole approach to foreign policy. What do you think the prospects of pulling that off are?

McNamara: Well, we started on the book tour two or three days ago, and we've been in New York and Philadelphia. People are initially shocked because a) they've never really thought about the killing in these terms and then b) when you say to them, "It's partially your responsibility to avoid that in this next century," they're shocked again.

They don't think they're responsible, but they are. We human beings have done it, and human beings can reduce it. I don't want to say we can completely stop it—I'm not naïve—but we can certainly reduce it.

GS: I want to ask you now about America's particular, and somewhat peculiar, position as the sole superpower of the world. I'm talking about the notion of American exceptionalism—of being somehow different and distinct from these kinds of considerations.

McNamara: Our leaders are stating it. We are the most powerful nation in the world—economically, politically, and militarily, no question about it. In that sense, we are exceptional.

But we tend to lead other people to believe that we think we're right, that we're omniscient, and by God, they better do what we say to do. Well, we're not always right. And if we can't persuade other nations with like values and interests to participate in the decisions and share the costs of what we're trying to do—both the financial costs and the blood costs—then we ought to reconsider our approach. If we had followed that approach we would not have been in Vietnam, because not one of our major allies—not Japan, France, Britain, or Germany—favored what we were doing there.

We do have to recognize that we are strong and, don't misunderstand me, that we have a responsibility to lead. I believe we should lead, but I don't believe we're always right, and I don't believe we should try to impose our will when other nations with comparable values and interests oppose us.

GS: I'm mindful of a very powerful point you made in the book, based on your experience during Vietnam with the opportunity to enlist Charles de Gaulle in negotiations with the North Vietnamese leadership, which might have changed the entire conflict. We didn't do it, though.

McNamara: A reason we didn't do it is what Dean Rusk said about de Gaulle: you go up on your hands and knees and you reach the throne and then he gives his wisdom. De Gaulle was an extremely difficult person to deal with and live with. Churchill found that out.

But he was also wise, and he was particularly wise and knowledgeable about Vietnam. And what he said was that you can form a neutral government. Now, we didn't think we could. But in hindsight, I think he was absolutely right. In the six meetings Jim Blight and I have had with what I call the Hanoi leaders—those who were with North Vietnam in the 1960s—they said we could have done it. De Gaulle said we could have done it. If we had gotten past our distaste for his particular approach, we could have made great use of that experience.

GS: This brings up another important point from the book, which is the utility in having the experience, the historical base, and the empathy to understand what the other side's reasons are—what their past and traditions are, and their motivation.

McNamara: Let me just say, so that your audience doesn't misinterpret me, that I don't consider empathy to be synonymous with sympathy, and I don't believe you would either. Empathy means trying to get inside the mind of the other person and trying to understand first, what they think, and second, why they think it, and third, how you can change it.

That's not the same thing as sympathy, but it does mean that we've got to spend more time trying to understand the way other people think and how they look at us.

In the book, I mention that in August of 1937 I was a merchant seaman in Shanghai, and I saw the Japanese start the Sino-Japanese War when they bombed Shanghai. Now, the Chinese haven't forgotten that. Li Peng, the former prime minister, told me two or three years ago that Japan caused the death, by that action and what followed, of 20 million Chinese. And he said that they have never apologized.

GS: And the importance of this is that even if that statistic is incorrect—

McNamara: That's the way they think. And that's what's going to be remembered and acted upon.

GS: And I don't think very many people or our policymakers are aware of the historical imperatives you just mentioned as a factor in the current Chinese reasoning.

McNamara: That's the problem. Li Peng also said, when I was meeting with him, "You've got to get all your troops out of foreign bases in the Pacific area."

I said, "Let me ask you something. What do you think would happen if we took all the troops out? Do you think we would continue to be able to provide the security guarantee to Japan?"

Well, he said, "That's for you to decide."

I said, "I asked you a question: you answer me, yes or no."

Again he said, "No, no, no—that's for you to decide."

So I said, "Let me tell you something. You know and I know you don't want Japan to be militarized. In a sense, many of them don't want to be militarized themselves, but if you force us to take all our troops out, we're not going to be able to provide a security guarantee. How the hell can we provide for their security if we don't have troops and bases? So you've got to answer the question."

Finally, he said, "Well, maybe for five years. Your security guarantee was to protect Japan in the Cold War against Russia. The Cold War has ended and Russia is no longer a threat. You still have the security treaty, and it's threatening us now."

I said, "You're totally wrong. You just answer the question: Do you want Japan to be militarized?"

He said, "No."

I said, "All right, well you better think about what we need to fulfill our obligations under this security treaty." So it is correct to say that they have to empathize with us.

GS: It's a two-way road.

McNamara: Absolutely. We need to communicate, and that's the lesson.

GS: What I think really drives *Wilson's Ghost* is a call to action for a new generation of leadership. It seems to me that people have to be educated differently about foreign policy and perhaps be different actors in carrying out this policy.

McNamara: You're absolutely correct, and this applies particularly to weapons. People have to be educated as to the risk of weapons of mass destruction—particularly nuclear weapons, which exist today and which we are not dealing with constructively.

GS: Another part of this re-education, if you will, has to do with globalization. We love to talk about globalization and the inter-dependent world, but that doesn't necessarily make it a safer place, does it?

McNamara: Not at all. Nor does it reduce the need for leadership. I think it does make both irresponsible and ineffective an attempt to direct the world unilaterally and force other people against their good judgment to accept our directions. They're not going to do that.

GS: I want to turn now to the slow motion nature of so many crises. Things sort of begin and then evolve, but if men and women were wise enough to arrest the development of the crisis at an early stage, it wouldn't become a catastrophe, would it?

McNamara: If you contrast Vietnam and the Cuban Missile Crisis, the Cuban Missile Crisis brought us within a hair's breadth of nuclear war. It was thirteen extraordinarily dangerous days. I didn't go home for thirteen days, and we hardly slept. But Vietnam extended over a quarter of a century, across five presidencies, and we never really got focused on it the way we should have.

GS: Your book points out something I never heard before. In response to a hypothetical question asked many years after, Fidel Castro said he would have gone to tactical nuclear use if he was compelled to do so.

McNamara: We did not know until thirty years after the Missile Crisis of October 1962. I was in Havana, in a meeting with Castro in 1992. We didn't know until that meeting, when the former Soviet commander of all the Warsaw Pact forces, the most senior military commander they had, told us he didn't realize he was telling us something we didn't know.

He told us there were tactical nuclear weapons and strategic nuclear weapons on the soil of Cuba on October 27, 1962. The majority of President Kennedy's military and civilian advisers were recommending an attack on Cuba. The CIA had said, "Well, of course we have photographs of the missiles, but we don't believe there are any nuclear warheads there. The first batch of twenty is coming on a ship named the *Poltava.*"

Thirty years later we learned they had 162—about 90 tactical warheads to be used against an invasion force and about 70 for the potential strategic attack on the east coast of the United States. We were that close to nuclear war.

So when this came out in Havana, I was totally shocked. I couldn't believe it. But finally we got it straightened out that we had heard correctly. General Anatoly Gribkov repeated what he'd said, and I said to Castro, "Mr. President, let me ask you three questions: One, did you know the nuclear weapons were there? Two, would you have favored their use in the event we attacked?

Three, if they had been used, what would have happened to Cuba?"

He said, "One, I did know they were there. Two, I not only would have—I did favor their use." He sent a cable to Khrushchev on Thursday the 25th of October before this critical Saturday recommending that in the event of an invasion they be used. And thirdly, he said, "Cuba would have been totally destroyed. Totally destroyed."

Then he said, "If you and Kennedy were facing the same, you would have done it." My God, I hope we wouldn't. Destroy the nation! Pull the temple down on our heads! That's the way they were thinking.

GS: That's a sobering moment indeed. On the question of Russia and China today, you make a very good case for empathy.

McNamara: People say it's absurd, because Russia and China are antagonistic and intend to hurt us. I counter that the two most important geopolitical events of the last half century, excluding only the end of the Cold War, were the reconciliation of France and Germany and the reconciliation between Japan and the United States after the bloodiest war in history.

Now by God, if France and Germany can reconcile, and if Japan and the United States can reconcile, to the point where there's virtually no chance of a war between any of these countries, why can't we integrate Russia and China in relations with the West?

GS: So it's a question of political will and of political spirit. The Wilson of your book, of course, is Woodrow Wilson. And in the post–World War I era we had that vindictive peace with Germany, which sowed the seeds for World War II.

McNamara: Wilson tried, and nearly killed himself trying, to avoid that, and then in addition, he tried to get us into the League of

Nations, and he failed on both. And that brought on World War II. We lost around 20 million during World War I and 50 million in World War II. It could have been avoided.

GS: The other point you're making, of course, is that the post–World War II spirit was entirely different, where enemies would reconcile. And if we were wise enough to reuse that in our approach to Russia and China, perhaps we would have a different outcome again.

It's not too late, but it may soon be. Communal violence: we see this everywhere from the Balkans to East Timor, Sierra Leone, Zaire, Bosnia, and Kosovo. It's a terrible list and it's growing. What's the key here? How does this country deal with other countries in meeting these challenges?

McNamara: It's very difficult, and I think the first point to make is that I believe Wilson was wrong.

GS: In self-determination?

McNamara: Yes. Wilson believed that the key to avoiding these communal violence conflicts was self-determination. But my God, could you have had self-determination in Bosnia or Kosovo? There are on the order of 5,000 ethnic groups in the world, but there are only on the order of 190 states, so you've got 40 ethnic groups in some states.

Now, are we going to allow each of those to self-determine their role in the future? No, we can't permit that. The violence will be greater. If we won't permit that, how are we going to deal with it?

We've got to develop some means for those who feel they're being penalized—the minorities being penalized by the majorities —to surface their complaints and have some tribunal or body to consider their complaints.

GS: You're calling for a viable, credible system of international justice that will give everyone the sense that they had their day in court.

McNamara: That's right. We don't have that now, and to the degree that efforts have been made to move in that direction, we have failed.

GS: So you think that a greater support for the United Nations, or an institution like that, is going to be vital in keeping this violence down.

McNamara: Just take the Security Council. It's totally ineffective. We're going to have to reorganize. In the first place, it's not representative. You don't have Germany involved. You don't have Japan involved. You don't have Brazil, Nigeria, or India. You've got to bring some of these large nations into the Security Council.

Secondly, the five permanent members have a veto power, and we, and Russia, and China exercise that veto power in rather unilateral ways. We've got to get rid of that. The American people will be very upset. I'm not suggesting that we're going to put ourselves in the hands of a lot of irrational, irresponsible members of the Security Council. Not at all.

If we give up the veto power for the permanent members, we've got to have some kind of qualified majority—let's say 75 percent of the permanent members have to vote in favor. But we must get rid of that veto power because China has, in a sense, prevented the Security Council from acting. Russia has prevented it from acting. Many times, we've prevented it from acting.

GS: Now, this book is based upon a moral philosophy. You advocate approaching these difficult international issues from a moral basis. It's not easy, is it?

McNamara: It's not easy, but I learned something when we were writing that book. I didn't know that all of the great religions of the world—Buddhism, Judaism, Christianity, the Orthodox Church, Hinduism, Islam—all of them share almost the exact same words: "Do unto others as you'd have them do unto you."

Some say that doesn't mean a damn thing because they don't apply it. Well, we don't always apply it either, but that's what we say we believe in. And the others say they believe it. So why don't we take them at their word and say, "Okay, look, you say we should treat others as we want them to treat us. We say that. And in this particular instance, no one is doing it."

GS: The book also contains a harrowing, if I may say so, and detailed description of what nuclear weapons do. These are not just bigger versions of other weapons.

McNamara: I put that in there because the average American doesn't understand it. So in the book we described the destructive power of a one megaton weapon, and then explained that a weapon only a hundredth the size of that destroyed Hiroshima.

And as we are talking here today, we have 7,500 strategic nuclear warheads targeted on Russia. Of the 7,500, 2,500 of them are on fifteen minute alert, and those 2,500 have a kill capability equal to 50,000 times that of the Hiroshima bomb. That's where we are. And the Russians have the same force targeted on us. This is insane.

GS: You call for the "zero option." That's the only option, right?

McNamara: That's right. We have 7,500 targeted on Russia today and they have 6,500 targeted on us. Well, President Bush just recently said, "We can unilaterally cut that force substantially." No other president has said that. I strongly agree with him on that.

Now how much would he cut it? He sort of pointed to 2,500 or 1,000. That would be a tremendous step. We're not by any means at the end, but that would be a major step forward. We all should support it.

GS: This is more than a book for you, isn't it? I mean, there's a sense of mission.

McNamara: Well, day after tomorrow I will be 85 years old, so you're damn right. It's sort of my last testament, and it's meant to be that.

Originally broadcast July 23, 2001.

3

Roméo Dallaire
Advancing Humanity by Transforming Peacekeeping Operations

Roméo Dallaire, who looks like a general out of central casting, served as force commander of the ill-fated United Nations peacekeeping force in Rwanda between 1993 and 1994. Dallaire made his best efforts to stop the genocide being waged by Hutu extremists against Tutsis but lacked the necessary troops. In 2000, he was diagnosed with post-traumatic stress disorder and spiraled into a deep depression. To move forward from those dark days, he wrote Shake Hands with the Devil, *a best seller, and now lectures widely on the lessons he learned in Rwanda.[1]*

�֍

George Seay: You said a number of times in the first chapters that you wrote this book to fill a void. What did you mean by that? What void are you seeking to fill?

Dallaire: There have been a number of scholarly and journalistic books written on Rwanda and the genocide by people who were not there at the time. The thrust of nearly all these publications

---

1. Roméo Dallaire, *Shake Hands with the Devil: The Failure of Humanity in Rwanda* (Carroll & Graf, 2004).

has been one of going back into history to the colonial and pre-colonial periods and then leaping into the actual genocide, while dissecting the different interplays of the world powers, the UN, NGOs, etc.

What I attempted to do with my book was to tell the story of an inside player—my reactions, my decisions, and what influenced me throughout that time frame. I produced no revisionism or Monday morning quarterbacking. I wrote what happened then and I spent a lot of time explaining the months leading up to the genocide as well as the genocide itself. I think that was the major vacuum.

GS: Your book also provides a lot of insight into what armies interested in peacekeeping and nation-building may be confronted with today. Is soldiering in the twenty-first century a different kind of enterprise and commitment?

Dallaire: We're now into a different scenario. We have the vestiges and responsibility of classic warfare still—nation against nation, with identifiable enemies and the use of all weapons—as we have the responsibility of protecting our nations.

However, this post–Cold War era that started nearly fifteen years ago has taught the military, not through formal process, but in fact through a kind of osmosis process, that war fighting is simply not enough. Being a warrior is just not enough. We now need also to be conflict resolvers. We need to be able to function in ambiguity. We need to be proactive in some of the most complex scenarios of peace and human rights, and ethical and moral dilemmas, that so many of these missions are bringing forward. You need a whole new set of skills.

The older, conservative crowd is saying, "If you fiddle in this softer stuff in a serious way, you will wear down the warrior ethic." My argument to that is that you need a balance between the two, and that the warrior ethic will not be attrited, because the warrior ethic is very much based on experiential aspects, while the soft skills of conflict resolution require a more intellectual basis. And so we're into quite a debate over the future of soldiering.

GS: It sounds to me like a sea change, in the sense that it calls for a greater sophistication from soldiers at every rank, from general to private, and for nations to understand that there are long-term commitments required—it's not just fight and leave.

Dallaire: That's right—the short-term exercises are over. If you're going to be in these conflict areas to support and assist them, you're in there for decades. And, in fact, creating artificial milestones like democratic elections in two years and so on merely exacerbates the complexities of the situation. We must evolve with these countries, as well as provide them with sustained support. We must not be paternalistic or neocolonialist in any way, shape, or form. And so the military dimension of that is in the midst of a revolution.

And as much as you're asking the soldiers to be intellectually strengthened, contrary to the old chain of command where the general knew everything and passed down the minimum of what soldiers needed to know, you now have a situation where the corporal on a barrier making the wrong decisions can scuttle the negotiations of an entire peace agreement for months.

GS: It makes me think that everyone—every rank, every man or woman in uniform—in those situations, is not only a soldier, but an ambassador, as well.

Dallaire: That's a rather interesting analogy because some of the skills we want them to have are precisely those of negotiation, patience, listening, and throwing out innovative ideas. And that's got to be done at the corporal level as much as the general level.

GS: I want to take us now back to those terrible moments when everything turned sour and the tragedy ensued in Rwanda. As I think any reasonable person would have to agree, the world community failed miserably. The central question, then, is why? Painful as the question may be, could it be that there's a perception that some people just aren't as important as others?

Dallaire: In the brutality of the genocide, I think you've also got to be brutal in the explanation and in bringing those facts forward. And in the brutality of it, Rwanda and Rwandans just didn't count. They were worth nothing to national interest. No strategic value, geography, or resources were there, and I was told that all that was there were humans and there were too many of them—it was overpopulated.

The reactions to the African killings, in contrast to the world's response to what happened in Yugoslavia, show that many do believe that some humans are more valuable than others. We don't want to incur casualties in trying to save Rwandans because we cannot handle those casualties. And so whether there's 100,000, 200,000, 300,000 Rwandans killed—it still does not warrant a decision to say that yes, it's important that we send people in to help, even if it means four, five, six, eight, or ten casualties of our own. That decision is simply unsustainable in the court of public opinion. But I believe that shedding blood of our own is crucial to the advancement of humanity and the respect of humanity, because it's simply not enough to respond to something because we want the oil, or strategic location, or whatever.

GS: At another important level, the book is obviously a moral story, and I want to actually quote something to give people a sense of that. This is early on when you're assessing things and trying to get your feet on the ground in terms of what the mission will need from the UN and so forth, and so you're talking to people. The passage begins, "I did not understand that I had just met men in Rwanda who would become *génocidaires* [genocidal killers]. While I thought I was the one who had been doing the assessing, I was the one who had been carefully measured. I still thought that for the most part people said what they meant." You go on to describe how these men with very sophisticated backgrounds obviously weren't saying what they meant.

And then you get to this riveting sentence at the end of that paragraph, where you say, "They knew us better than we knew ourselves." Talk to me about that.

Dallaire: One of the terrible things we do from our haughty positions in the developed world is to consider the people in the nondeveloped world dummies. In fact, their sophistication was not limited to the intellectual, but extended to the practical as well—how to influence international public opinion, and how to maneuver the country to their own best advantage, even operating as the hardliners and extremists in a totally nonethical scenario.

They knew exactly what they were doing, and we, in good faith, operating under the context that both sides wanted the peace agreement, and that they wanted a neutral force, a referee, were prepared to conduct these operations within that dimension. I accuse myself particularly of failing in the mission, and one of the dimensions of this was my naïveté of the sophistication that existed on the ground.

I was thirty years into the army at that point, and yet, we were all totally Eurocentric. Operations in northern Norway—I come from Nordic country—were no problem. Operating in the central European front was no problem. However, going into the sophistication of conflict resolution in countries where the geography is foreign and more importantly, the whole cultural aspect of what makes these people tick was totally nonexistent, was a whole new challenge.

All of a sudden, I discovered that in a number of meetings, although the person in front of me had a significant amount of authority, rarely was that person calling the shots. It was the person in the second or third row who had the control and the power. And when you had a break or something, there wasn't any rush to that person—it was all done in a very subtle fashion.

GS: I was appalled when I realized the paucity of resources that you go into these kinds of conflicts with. You were basically fighting for stationery and stamps to get these things under way. It was no well-heeled operation.

Because there seemed to be so little money and so much bureaucracy, you were also compelled to, as you say, "situate the estimate." In other words, you know what you need, but you know you're not going to get it, so you work with a figure you know you can get and make the best of it.

Despite all these, and many other, disappointments, you still seem to be a very strong believer in the UN. Why is that, and what do you think it should do?

Dallaire: I think the UN, with all its weaknesses, is still the only impartial and transparent organization in the world. Between the UN and all its complexities, and single-nation-led coalitions— usually led by big superpowers—I'll prefer the UN, because the fundamental motive behind the UN is its charter, and that charter is humanity and human rights. Single-nation-led coalitions are dominated by self-interest, national interest—too often, what we can do for humanity is simply a byproduct.

The other aspect of it is that in the UN, you have the potential for innovative thinking and innovative solutions. You have the opportunity to marry the complex diplomatic exercises and complex security analyses coming from the orchestra of the world.

The hope is that the orchestra is made up of different sections, but that these sections are able to come together to produce music. That doesn't exist as clearly and as evidently outside the UN. What is emasculating the UN still today is the fact that we don't want to give it the full rein.

The example I use is the Iraq scenario. We spent fifty years in NATO working together against the Warsaw Pact. Yet the debate on Iraq split us like it never split us during NATO. How is that possible?

I believe one of the reasons is that we didn't give full opportunity for the diversity of diplomatic or political solutions to run their course. Middle powers were not given room to bring forward ideas and found it difficult to find niches amongst the big powers. And the big powers ended up tripping over each other because, to my sorrow, there isn't a statesman among them—only a lot of politicians and egos.

GS: In this time of insecurity that we both believe is the most dangerous time we've ever seen, how do we create a constituency for humanity?

Dallaire: The first point is that we've got to consider this to be a long-term activity. I personally will work for the rest of my life discussing the Rwandan genocide and what lessons it can provide to advance humanity. But I think it may be three or four centuries from now before we'll actually stop conflict because of our differences. Then it won't exist anymore. But that will mean that we're working at it every day, and it means that millions will still die as we make our way toward that.

I believe the instrument to move that way is the maturing of the NGO community. Nongovernmental organizations are considered still to be very immature and disparate, and as such are not yet able to fully influence nation-states that continue to debate whether or not things like sovereignty are absolutes. Sovereignty is one of the biggest impediments to us being able to intervene in order to be proactive and anticipatory. So I think it's important to embrace the NGO community, which is motivated by humanity and human rights, and its potential.

Originally broadcast August 16, 2004.

4

Alma Guillermoprieto
Latin America's Great Guerrilla Epic

*Alma Guillermoprieto, a Mexican journalist who has written
widely for the British and American press, has presence—a
quiet, poetic magnetism borne of empathy for the lives of real
people. In 1982 she was one of two reporters to break the story
on the El Mozote massacre in El Salvador, in which some 900
villagers were slaughtered by the Salvadoran army. She has also
covered the Colombian civil war, the Shining Path rebels in Peru,
and post-Sandinista Nicaragua, and is widely considered an
expert on the politics and culture of Latin America during the
"lost decade."*

※

George Seay: I've read your great writing for many years, Alma.
You use a phrase in *Looking for History* that I think makes an
important contribution to the subject matter.[1] You note that
you are striving to "reveal the hidden and enigmatic aspects of
Latin American history and culture." Reading the book, one gets
the distinct impression that there exists too much discussion on,
and policy decisions about, the region without being informed
by that.

---

1. Alma Guillermoprieto, *Looking for History: Dispatches from Latin America* (Pantheon,
2001).

Guillermoprieto: Policy discussion and policymaking tend to be about chess and not about people. What I try to do in the book is talk about the societies and the people living through these processes without excessive reference to the policies themselves. There is a sense in which I am not interested in that. I am interested in what happened to people. I think there might be some ideal combination of the two which would improve things for everybody.

Unfortunately, understanding people and their actual lives is so much more difficult and time-consuming than thinking about policies conceptually. In fairness to policymakers, they often don't have the time it requires. They have to turn in their reports and hurry to resolve situations. What I'm talking about is a luxury, in many ways.

GS: History, culture, literature, society—these are extremely important in Latin America, aren't they?

Guillermoprieto: I think so, and this is one of the things I'm trying to puzzle out in the book: What is the interplay between historical history, remembered history, and current reality? One of the reasons literature is so strong in Latin America is because events tend to be remembered through the filter of memory, rather than through the reporting of facts. Perhaps that's a result of the fact that we don't have such a strong journalistic tradition, so we're not obsessed with wondering if something really happened exactly that way. Instead, we think about how *we* remember it, and how it affected our lives.

GS: As you said that, names flashed through my mind—Gabriel García Márquez, Mario Vargas Llosa—those writers and many others who deal with memory in history this way.

Guillermoprieto: I think that is the Latin American novelistic tradition, and when that kind of magical realism boom burst upon the world in the early- to mid-sixties, it was received with such joy by readers because it was like being allowed to live life through somebody else's dreams.

GS: Your articles and dispatches and essays in this book introduce us through this perspective to countries like Colombia, Cuba, Mexico, and Peru. With Colombia, you introduce us to the extraordinary, dramatic story of FARC,[2] the leftist guerrilla group. There's much to be said about this, but one thing I was immediately struck by was how young the fighters were. It almost seemed to be a children's war. These are basically young teenagers.

Guillermoprieto: Yes. I don't know that I would say it is a children's war, because I think the connotations of that in today's climate might get people very excited and indignant, and I think we should probably be striving to get people to become *less* excited and indignant.

But it is definitely a teenagers' war. The FARC is a very old organization. It is perhaps the oldest guerrilla organization in the world, operating since the late 1950s and under its present name, since the early 1960s. The paradox is that it has very old leadership. Its leader is Manuel Marulanda, and he's now seventy-two or seventy-three years old, which makes him the world's oldest living guerrilla. But his army is one composed of

---

2. *Fuerzas Armadas Revolucionarias de Colombia* (Revolutionary Armed Forces of Colombia).

very, very young men and women. (About 30 percent of the total FARC forces are girls.)

Why are they so young? I think partly it is because in Colombia's geography, the sheer physical endurance you need to get through a day of combat or cross-country march demands that you be really young. I did it once and it nearly killed me.

GS: And what is it that motivates these young kids? Is it reverence for these older figures? Is it ideology? Because this conflict has lasted a very long time now.

Guillermoprieto: Yes it has; we're going on forty years now. Reverence for the leadership is one factor, yes, although I didn't really see any traces of a personality cult. You would have expected that, but it's not there, although Marulanda is revered. Still, it's not "Let us praise our great leader, Marulanda!"

I think a lot of it is the enormous resentment of Colombian back-country people toward the arrogant owning classes in the cities. I think that has been a very powerful motivating force, as well as the fight for land. I also think there is a tradition of violence in Colombia. The society and its leaders have never found a way to create a reasonably peaceful and reasonably just society that can incorporate its poor.

The other thing is—and I know you've been to Colombia, so maybe you'll agree—the enormous seductiveness of Colombia. The reason why so many of us go there and just fall in love with it despite the violence and chaos is a sense of liberty in a place that is so chaotic. Teenagers in the United States dream of that kind of liberty by listening to rock and roll and pretending to act bad. Colombian teenagers get to act bad if they join the guerrillas, or even if they join the paramilitaries, for that matter.

GS: It's a kind of self-affirmation.

Guillermoprieto: It's self-affirmation. It's carry a gun. It's being powerful, which of course is every teenager's dream.

GS: Another thing that occurred to me is that the resentment of those in desperate circumstances toward those in the chattering rich classes in the urban areas exists throughout the region. It's continent-wide, isn't it?

Guillermoprieto: Oh yes. The big question is why Colombia has never been able to deal with it. And I think it has to do again with that extraordinary up-and-down geography. It's like the Stairmaster of countries—you never finish climbing up or going down.

Along with the geography, there also was never a period when a real society could stabilize and form. All other countries, at some point, have had that privilege—usually through a dictator, remarkably enough. Colombia hasn't even had that; it's too chaotic even for that.

GS: There's an American dimension to this, too. President Bill Clinton designed a $1.3 billion aid package for Colombia, and the current George W. Bush administration is carrying it forward. Now of course, in the American context, it was presented as an "anti-narcotics effort," but right from the start a lot of people were scratching their heads, wondering how this kind of effort was even feasible in a country with a guerrilla war like Colombia's.

Guillermoprieto: Certainly. There's a lot of slippage in that definition of the aid package's purpose, isn't there?

GS: Well, that's the question, Alma. Do you think the slippage is becoming more pronounced?

Guillermoprieto: I think intentionally so, yes. And I think in the same way that September 11th managed to change everything else in the world, it has changed the situation in Colombia, because the current administration has incorporated the FARC into its list of terrorist organizations and has made a very clear policy decision to change definitions in a way that will allow the anti-drug money to be used for anti-guerrilla combat.

There is additional funding, as well, and I think that's what I find most startling. There is an additional $98 million being appropriated right now, supposedly for the defense of U.S. interests in Colombia. The appropriation lists three geographical points where American interests might have to be defended, though I have not seen the list.

GS: On the other side, I'm bemused by FARC's most recent kidnappings and the tactics we're seeing. Frankly, I don't understand the logic.

Guillermoprieto: Again, I think that September 11th had a great deal to do with FARC's decision to give up on the peace talks. Since the beginning of this year, they had essentially been looking for a way to break off the peace talks without looking like they were the ones taking the offensive. I'm not sure it worked very well, but the peace talks are broken and there is now war in the country.

What do I think happened? I think that after September 11th and the various military initiatives taken around the world by the United States, as well as the administration's decision to list the FARC as a terrorist organization, the FARC looked at the situation, as well as the rise in the polls of a Colombian presidential candidate who was staunchly anti-guerrilla, and decided, "This isn't going to get any better."

GS: So, let's bring things to a kind of ultimate confrontation.

Guillermoprieto: Yes. "Let's start the confrontation again. We've been doing these peace talks for three years. There's no point in continuing. We might be getting soft. And if it's going to be time for war again, well then, let's get going."

GS: It's both frightening and fascinating. I want to turn now, Alma, to the individuals in your book, because so much of the book is about individuals and not just countries. The individuals in your book have names that many Americans and worldwide audiences recognize: Che, Evita, Mario Vargas Llosa. Let's begin with Che. You use a phrase for him that I want to get you to comment on. You call him "the century's first Latin American."

Guillermoprieto: It's sort of terrible, isn't it, that the century's first Latin American would achieve the renown that he did by feeling like he had to resort to violence to call the world's attention to Latin America. It also says something about Latin Americans' isolation. Argentineans don't care all that much about Mexico. Mexicans don't follow Colombian news. Che assumed he wasn't Argentinean, or Cuban, but that he was Latin American. That we were a cultural unity. That we were a social unity. And I think that was at least part of the source of his great and enduring appeal.

GS: I have always thought of Che, and your account confirmed this, that he is a natural soldier and leader. He's a middle class kid from Buenos Aires, he's asthmatic, and he becomes a doctor. But he has this compulsion with machismo all his life, I think. It seems to me to be a bit of a strength and a limitation. He really is a soldier, but I never have gotten a sense of much nuance in the mind of Ernesto "Che" Guevara.

Guillermoprieto: I didn't either. I think all soldiers turned politicians tend to find themselves confronted with their own rigidity, and their own understanding of why people just won't obey.

They ask themselves, "Why don't they understand that what I'm saying is what they should be doing and what's good for them?"

Well, it's because societies don't work like armies.

GS: It's messier.

Guillermoprieto: That's right; it's messier. It gets tangled. It's complicated. It's like trying to herd kittens. People just go off every which way. Another tragic thing about Che is that he couldn't deal with other people's failings, and he couldn't deal with his own. And the terrible thing about Che's life is that he goes off in pursuit of what's best so that he can feel that he's redeemed himself.

GS: Those last chapters of his life really were a descent.

Guillermoprieto: Into hell.

GS: I was in Brazil living and working in the countryside when he was killed in Bolivia, and I remember a peasant woman who looked upon his picture, and she said, "He has the face of Christ." I remember that quote.

Guillermoprieto: Yes, and that image stuck with us forever because, in fact, that woman was right. He does look like a Christ figure there—somebody who died for our sins, but who also died for his own sins because he couldn't forgive himself. And as a result of that lack of flexibility—that lack of capacity to be tolerant with himself—I think he closed doors in Latin America that should have remained open for discussion, for negotiation, for finding maybe not the perfect answer but the least unsatisfactory answer for all sides. He opened the doors to Latin America's great guerrilla epic, which of course has been tragic and moving, but not necessarily effective.

GS: I want to turn now to the chapters on Cuba, which are very revealing. I wrote in my notes that Cuba is courting dollars, papal approval, and continued popular support. It's therefore an unusual mixture of communism and materialism, even as its charismatic leader is aging. Is this a very fragile, dramatic moment for Cuba culturally?

Guillermoprieto: That's absolutely accurate. It is a fragile, dramatic moment. The waning days of a regime are always tragic because there's a loss of inner faith. The terrible dilemma that Cubans face at this moment is that after forty years of revolution, they don't have much to show for it. The world has been becoming increasingly materialistic. They have access to television programs, access to radio stations, and they get bombarded like everyone in the rest of the world does by consumerism and demand to acquire material goods, because if you don't have a lot of stuff, you're nobody. And in that context, Cubans are really poor and don't have anything after forty years of sacrifice and struggle.

And so I think the self-questioning going on—"What did we do all of this for? What does it add up to? What will we be worth in this new world we're coming to after Fidel dies?"—is a very dramatic situation. Fidel is an old man now; he'll be gone sometime in the foreseeable future. Cubans are wondering, "What next? What happens with my great skills in Bulgarian and Russian? What use can I put those to?"

GS: One reaction I have to all this is that I don't think Raoul Castro is going to succeed him.

Guillermoprieto: Somehow, I think you're right. It's just not happening. He is not charismatic. He is not original. He is not forceful. And he stands in his brother's enormous shadow. Whoever would be a worthy successor would have to be as gigantic as Fidel has been throughout his years in power. That's not happening.

GS: I tried just now to imagine myself a Cuban of a certain age, roughly my own, and I think I might say, "Well, I'm also very proud because I stood against Goliath and we're still here." And I would still think that people would want to protect that. They have a place in the world and it really is unique in that sense.

Guillermoprieto: I hope that all that is preserved. I very much doubt it. I think that in today's world economy, money and buying power really are hugely important, and the island Cubans are going to be faced with the arrival of the Florida Cubans, who have a right to their country land (and I'll note that they have every right to come back), and who are going to return with a lot more money and a lot more ability to deal with the modern world. They have management skills. And I think that's going to be a very painful confrontation. Worse probably than the mis-encounter between the East and West Germans.

It's not going to be easy. It's going to be painful. But it has to happen and I think that one of the things that Fidel must be held accountable for is that he has held back the development of Cuba for probably the last twenty years. There has been no originality in his thinking or in his way of approaching the country's problems.

GS: So Cuba is therefore unprepared for the transition.

Guillermoprieto: Right. There's a lot of dammed up history that is going to have to be resolved overnight with very little preparation.

GS: Let's move on to another individual you write so well about, Alma, and that is Mario Vargas Llosa. He's one of the world's greatest writers and a man who ran for the presidency of Peru in 1990. His candidacy was doing very well for a while and then it fell apart. It plummeted. And I think lots of people—myself included—were scratching our heads and wondering why this had happened. I thought you had a marvelous quote in your book about this when you wrote, "It seemed to lack the perception of his novels." I was struck by that. Here's a man whose novels are wonderful depictions of Peru, and yet the campaign he ran was not Peru.

Guillermoprieto: It's interesting to me always, the vision in the mind of the artist. What the novelist knows and what the aspiring politician knows seem to be two very different things. Vargas Llosa, as a novelist, has really written more insightfully and more intimately about Peru than any other Peruvian writer, but as a politician he was inept and also unschooled. He didn't understand politics and he didn't understand what people looked for in their politicians. He thought what they wanted was somebody who would tell them what was right, and that's not what people want.

He felt he was going to give them a sense of order and what people really look for in politicians is a sense of purpose. Or at least in Latin America. At any rate, I'm reminded very much of my editor at Knopf, of all people, who when I first started writing and thought that maybe I ought to go off and do something different—you know, go to Russia, learn Russian, anything at all—said to me, "Just because you're doing something and doing it well doesn't mean it's not worth doing."

And I would have repeated that mantra to Mario Vargas Llosa when he decided that being a novelist wasn't good enough and that what he had to do was go and be a politician.

GS: So his mistake was reinventing himself.

Guillermoprieto: I think his mistake was not realizing how important he was to the world as a novelist. He thought, "Oh well, I do that brilliantly—that's easy. Time to stop. And why not do this other thing that I've never tried?" I hope that he saw it as a great adventure, because then maybe he can laugh about the great failure that it actually was.

GS: As a failure, as a great failure, which I also hope he can laugh about now, does it also give us something of an insight into the role of the intellectual in Latin American politics today? Because what Mario did in 1991 has a long tradition. Latin American intellectuals, as we both know, in all countries, have worn several hats and gone in and out of politics and so forth. Is there a lesson for the writers of today in light of this?

Guillermoprieto: I think that the lesson is that intellectuals are very important for people living in Latin America because, to start with, they have this great skill of knowing how to read and write fluently and fluidly, which is admired. And so they're often looked to for opinions, and to speak out against dictatorships and injustice. And many people wind up respecting the intellectuals because they are always questioning power.

GS: As we come to the end of our conversation, I do not want to give Mexico short shrift because it's a big country and your essays and dispatches on the country are riveting, but we only have a few moments remaining. Have we seen the end of an era, in a sense? Vicente Fox had his dramatic victory over PRI,[3] who had ruled for seventy-one years, I think. When I lived in Mexico, I thought they never would lose.

Guillermoprieto: I think that the whole issue of getting rid of the PRI was convincing voters that the PRI *could* lose, because like you, so many of us were convinced that it was eternal. And then it turned out to be Humpty Dumpty. Now that it's fallen off the wall, I don't think it will ever be able to put itself back together again—at least not in its past form where we relied on it to think for us and rule for us and take care of those nasty problems like accounting and paying the rent that we didn't want to be bothered with.

Originally broadcast April 15, 2002.

---

3. *Partido Revolucionario Institucional* (Institutional Revolutionary Party). Fox defeated the PRI candidate in the 2000 presidential elections.

5

Saad Eddin Ibrahim
Democratic Reform in Egypt

*Saad Eddin Ibrahim is one of Egypt's best-known dissident
intellectuals. Founder of the reformist Ibn Khaldun Center
for Development Studies at the American University of Cairo,
he was jailed, along with 27 of his colleagues, in June 2000 by
the Egyptian authorities. In prison, too, he was a leader, serving
as counselor, mailman, letter writer, even psychiatrist. After three
years, all charges were dismissed and Ibrahim was set free. I learned
from him that humor is an essential component of courage, for
although his story is grim, he delivered it with a twinkle. Today, he
remains just as vocal on human rights issues in Egypt as ever.*

❋

George Seay: You've gone through this experience of being
incarcerated in Egypt for your work on human rights, and your
release has been widely welcomed. I guess what I want to know
is whether you consider your release an individual act, or is there
a wider significance in it for the human rights community in
Egypt and elsewhere?

Ibrahim: I would like to think that there is wider significance.
Just as my arrest and incarceration had rippling effects across the
entire civil society and human rights community in my country,
Egypt, so did my release and my acquittal. I like to think of what

happened to me as symptomatic of the battle—an ongoing battle—rounds of which we win, rounds of which we lose. But the battle is on. And so long as there is a fighting chance, I think there is reason to be optimistic about the future of democracy.

GS: Your commitment to your causes is very clear, and has been throughout your life, as well as what I think of as your philosophical acceptance of what one must deal with in life. I've heard some very interesting stories that even in prison, you were something of a communicator. Is that correct?

Ibrahim: It is. It was part of a self-interested attempt to maintain my sanity and to maintain my sociability, because the worst thing that can happen to you is to have your soul defeated in prison. Being put in solitary confinement was meant to do that—to reduce my humanity, to diminish my humanity, and to prevent me from communicating with others. And so it became almost like a minor holy crusade to communicate with others and to maintain my mind.

I have to thank all those inmates—about 500 of them in my particular prison. Despite my solitary confinement, many of them, if not all of them, found ways of communicating with me.

GS: Dr. Ibrahim, give us a sense of what the most pressing human rights issues are in Egypt today. We in the West tend to think of issues like women's suffrage and judicial reform. Are those the rights issues that concern you most at this moment in Egypt?

Ibrahim: Well, those definitely are part of the concern, but the most important issue right now is to release political detainees from prison—those in Egypt and elsewhere in the Middle East. Second is to engage seriously in political reform, because that would be the ultimate safeguard against a repeat of human rights violations. So these are two structural things that must be done immediately, and which I consider most pressing.

GS: When you say "structural things," it sounds to me like you and your colleagues at the Ibn Khaldun Center want to get to the root of the problems, the causes of them, rather than the symptoms.

Ibrahim: That is precisely correct.

GS: And so when you talk about political reform, give us an idea of what you mean by that.

Ibrahim: The constitutions of Egypt and several other Middle Eastern countries look very good on paper. However, there are two or three articles that undermine all the good aspects of the constitution. One is the fact that there is no limit on presidential tenure in office, so some of the presidents have remained in power for as long as thirty years, unchallenged.

Second, officials resort to referendum rather than competitive elections. Third, the presidents in many of the Middle Eastern countries have amassed tremendous amounts of power in their offices, at the expense of both the judiciary and legislative branches of government. These are three important things that have to be corrected, and once they are resolved, the rest can come in due time.

GS: Is it your sense that popular opinion would welcome these kinds of reforms?

Ibrahim: Oh yes. This is a longstanding demand. It's not just the politically organized. This has been a popular demand for so long, and let me assure you that if it succeeds in a country like Egypt, it will help the democratization of Iraq and elsewhere in the

Middle East. Egypt is a pivotal country. As President George W. Bush said last week, Egypt has been a leader in the peace process with Israel, and it should also be a leader in political reform.

GS: I know that the Ibn Khaldun Center is at the forefront of this effort, and I assume there are other nongovernmental organizations in Egypt similarly employed.

Ibrahim: Absolutely.

GS: But you know, as I read about Ibn Khaldun, am I correct that you chose to create it as a commercial enterprise in order to get around of some of the onerous requirements placed upon NGOs in Egypt?

Ibrahim: We call the form "civil company." It's not commercial in the sense that we do not deal in commodities, but a civil company is a legal form we stumbled across in one of the very obscure articles of the Egyptian civil court.

We used this obscure article, and it is the one that ultimately got us acquitted, because we were doing things legally, within the bounds of the law. Similar organizations have emulated it, and when the government wants to crack down on them, they refer to the article.

Of course, being a civil company, we have to pay taxes if our revenues exceed our expenses. We have gladly paid taxes on any surplus, which was always very little, anyhow. As you know, these organizations don't make much money. But paying taxes to buy freedom was welcomed. After all, this is how other democratic revolutions have started.

GS: With "No taxation without representation."

Ibrahim: No taxation without representation.

GS: I appreciate that answer for a number of reasons. One is that it illustrates how you have to intelligently form your institution to start with. But what does it tell us about the prospects for nongovernmental organizations in general? Is it any easier to create them now, and how important are they?

Ibrahim: They are very important, because we consider NGOs the tissues of civil society. They are the living nerves of civil society. And civil society is the infrastructure for any democracy, because that's where you learn all the democratic skills—how to organize, how to dialogue, how to debate, how to get things done, how to mobilize, how to practice your rights as a citizen.

You learn these things on a smaller scale at an NGO or a civil society organization, and you therefore become better prepared for practicing those rights as a citizen in the polity at large.

You know, Egypt had a very vibrant civil society during the liberal age, up until 1952. But then came the populist regime of the late President Gamal Abdel Nasser, and civil society was emasculated. Now, we're trying to revive it, and we think its revival is imperative for any sustainable democratic reform.

GS: When you spoke of the polity of Egypt, something struck my mind, and that is the demographics of Egypt. I have a perception of Egypt, like many countries in the Middle East, having a vast and growing number of young people. It seems as though young people are particularly interested in reform, because it promises greater expression and employment and so forth. So the question that intrigues me is whether you think that the pace of reform is keeping pace with the aspirations of Egypt's youth?

Ibrahim: No, it is not. If it was, I probably wouldn't be as involved as I am, and I wouldn't have been in prison. No, it is definitely not. There is a lag and there is a gap, and there is a real crisis. And we are trying peacefully to convince our regime to address these issues, and we hope they will listen and hope that this ongoing dialogue will succeed in getting the ruling party and the government to initiate real reform, not just cosmetic reform.

GS: Do you think they are feeling the pressure?

Ibrahim: We like to think that after the war in Iraq, there is enough pressure in the region that all regimes, not just the Egyptian regime, will take note and will initiate changes, and if they don't, they are broadly courting some dark consequences.

I don't want to be in the doomsday business, because I'm an optimistic person and I think it can be done. I am encouraged by what happened in Morocco, in Turkey, in Bahrain, and even in Saudi Arabia, which announced elections on the local level. So the reforms are starting. And if countries which came from far behind where Egypt is have initiated these kinds of forceful steps toward democratization, then I'm hopeful that bigger countries like Egypt or Syria will follow suit, and hopefully Iraq will succeed as well.

GS: You seem to be saying that there is a fluid situation brought about by the events in Iraq that other governments in the region would be well advised to take advantage of. The war is viewed here in America in very controversial terms, but you see some openings perhaps.

Ibrahim: I do indeed. Iraq had a liberal age between 1920 and 1958, so in the collective memory of Iraqis, people over the age of forty or fifty remember having a liberal age, a multiparty political system, a parliament, lively debates in which a prime minister could be a Shia or a Sunni or a Kurd and nobody would blink, because the country was not attuned to think in sectarian terms. Now, that kind of civil society has a good chance of being revived. I don't want to be too rosy and suggest that it can be done overnight, but if we have that faith and that reading of Iraqi history, or Egyptian history for that matter, we should be able to build on that collective liberal legacy.

GS: That answer reminds us all that there is a rich tradition in the Middle East, and an awful lot of talent and energy. And because you are a scholar and an intellectual, let me ask you if you think the intellectual community is doing what it should be doing to advance these causes. Are they writing enough, speaking enough, both to each other and, perhaps more importantly, to the outside world? Are Arab intellectuals conversing the way you would like them to on these questions?

Ibrahim: Unfortunately, not enough. In several Middle Eastern countries, there's been a protracted reign of terror that has frightened intellectuals, intimidated them, and prevented them from emerging as a cohesive community. Also, many were used by the regime and tempted to come to power. And, of course, some of them took the bait and rushed and competed to be in power, which created a lot of suspicion.

However, we at the Ibn Khaldun Center have put the questions to Arab intellectuals. Would we initiate change ourselves, with our own hands, with our free will, or are we going to wait until it is imposed on us by a superpower from the outside? That triggered a very healthy debate and that debate is going on. And this is probably the beginning of restoring discourse to the Arab intellectual community.

GS: You wrote a piece in the *Washington Post* about the Israeli and Palestinian conflict in which you outlined a roadmap not just for those groups, but for the region as a whole. Tell us about that.

Ibrahim: The roadmap was universally welcomed by the quartet —Western Europe, Russia, the United States, and the UN—and there was some good will at the time to implement it. But it ran into all kinds of roadblocks.

But before it ran into roadblocks, I was, in my typical optimistic way, calling for a roadmap for the whole region, a roadmap of reform for every country in the region because of my firm belief that the Palestinian-Israeli issue runs into trouble because of lack of democracy in the neighboring countries.

Democracy and peace become two faces of the same coin. Immanuel Kant, the German philosopher, said some two hundred years ago that democracies do not go to war with each other. So I believe that by establishing democracies around Palestine, and hopefully in Palestine as well, we will create the best safeguard against derailing the peace process.

GS: Every time I speak to people from the region, they almost always say that the Palestinian-Israeli conflict really is the most central issue of the region. Do you see it that way?

Ibrahim: It is. However, I refuse to keep the rest of the region's issues hostage to that conflict. The Palestinian question to the Arabs is like the Jewish question in Western civilization. The Jewish question remained agonizing in Western Europe, and in the West in general, until the state of Israel was created. And even with that, the question has not disappeared.

The fate of the Palestinians weighs very heavily on the conscience of Arabs, of Muslims, and of the Third World. Their fate remains a constant reminder of the betrayal by the West, and that is why, as long as this problem is not seriously addressed, the credibility of America and the West is always in question.

GS: If we could wave a magic wand for a moment, and we suddenly got what we wanted on that issue and there was great progress, would that open up opportunities in the rest of the region?

Ibrahim: Absolutely. I remember being in prison when Camp David II took place, and I read it. When I read what they arrived at, I was optimistic, and I immediately wrote and smuggled my views out of prison, and it was actually printed in, of all places, a Saudi Arabian daily newspaper. I urged the Palestinians and the Arabs to accept the bargains struck at Camp David. I anticipated that many leaders would be hesitant or intimidated or afraid to put their backing behind it. I said that one way of settling this and dissipating the fears that some of the leaders may have had would be to put that package to a referendum, to both the Palestinians and the Israelis, so that Mr. Ariel Sharon and Mr. Yasser Arafat would not have a monopoly over whether or not to endorse the Camp David package. And here is where democracy is important. I think people are fatigued, both in Israel and in Palestine, because of this endless bloodshed that has claimed so many Jewish and Palestinian lives.

And it is becoming the new apartheid. Apartheid ended in South Africa, but we have a new apartheid in Palestine with the building of that wall. We get rid of the Berlin Wall, and here is Mr. Sharon building another wall. This is disturbing, and should be disturbing to every freedom lover in the world.

GS: I want lastly to ask you about attitudes toward America, particularly in Egypt. Americans are always concerned about anti-Americanism in particular. What's your sense of how Egypt looks at America?

Ibrahim: Well, if you go by the media, which are state-controlled and popularly viewed in the big cities, you'll find lots of anti-Americanism and a negative image of America. However, I have submitted that this is a surface feeling, and that deep down, there is still admiration for America and for the United States, and most of the anti-Americanism is really against foreign policy, not against the American people or the American way of life, as evidenced by the long lines in front of every American embassy or consulate, with people wanting visas to come, to visit, to trade, to study, to get American treatment.

There is enormous demand for American-style education. Even in our region, whenever an American-like university opens, there is a tremendous amount of demand for it. So the anti-Americanism which appears on the surface is very thin and could easily be diminished should American foreign policy correct itself and get back on track and give us a push to democratize the region.

Originally broadcast November 26, 2003.

6

Nayereh Tohidi, Lilia Labidi, and Haleh Esfandiari

Finding Feminism in Islam

In spring 2002, three Wilson Center scholars focused on women's issues in the Islamic world. Nayereh Tohidi, professor and chair of women's studies at California State University, Northridge, was a Kennan Institute research scholar studying women in Azerbaijan. Lilia Labidi, professor of psychology and anthropology at the University of Tunis, was a fellow studying public morality in the Arab world and North Africa. And Haleh Esfandiari, author of Reconstructed Lives: Women and Iran's Islamic Revolution, *is director of the Center's Middle East Program.[1]*

※

George Seay: As America and the West direct more attention to understanding Islam and the societies of the Islamic world, the current place of women in those societies and their future prospects assume critical importance. It's a very complex topic, so I'm pleased to be discussing those topics today with three distinguished scholars and authors.

I like to begin topics like this one in the most provocative way

---

1. Haleh Esfandiari, *Reconstructed Lives: Women and Iran's Islamic Revolution* (Woodrow Wilson Center Press, 1997).

possible. With that in mind, I want to introduce the term "Islamic feminism" to the conversation and ask you, Nayereh, to explain what that term means and—more importantly—what your reaction to it is.

Tohidi: As you said, even the very term itself is controversial and provocative. Two groups of people have the strongest opposition to it. One is the right-wing, conservative fundamentalists, who see no compatibility between Islam and feminism, and thus don't want to mix the two. The second group of people who see the term as a kind of oxymoron is made up of ultra-leftist secularists who are very anti-Islam and don't want to mix those two.

Nayereh Tohidi

GS: So there exists opposition from both the right and left extremes.

Tohidi: Precisely. In reality, "Islamic feminism" is a new movement that emerged about two decades ago. Most of the Muslim women in this reform movement are urbanized, highly educated, and middle class. Many are career-oriented, professional women who use Islam as a framework for empowering themselves, and who are trying to take away the monopoly of interpretation of Islam from the male clerics.

GS: And do they turn to the Koran for theological interpretation that justifies their concept of feminism?

Tohidi: Yes. Like any other modernist, reformist trend within Islam, Muslim feminism is very Koran-centered. By that I mean, they want to put aside other sources of Islam which are less reliable and more tainted with political interpretations than the Koran itself. They concentrate on the Koran as the foundation for Islamic understanding and Islamic community. But the Koran—like any other religious text—is almost silent until you read it. We read texts based on our presuppositions, and since modern presuppositions are different—especially with regard to women and gender roles—from the ones we had decades and centuries ago, their interpretation of the Koran's meaning is fundamentally different and centered around a woman's point of view. They want to reclaim Islam for women; they see the norms of God at odds with the norms of society.

GS: Listening to you, I can't help but think that this is compatible with secular feminism, in that these are the rights and privileges that women anywhere in the world want. With that, Lilia, I want to turn the conversation to your country, Tunisia, which is one of the most progressive countries in the world in that regard. Can you give us a sense of how feminism developed in Tunisia in general, and of family law in particular?

Labidi: The case of Tunisia is a little unusual. To understand the code of family, we have to look at the society and what has happened during this century. Tunisia, like Egypt, has had a great feminist movement throughout the twentieth century. Debate about the condition of women and family was very strong in Egypt, as in Tunisia. But the difference between Tunisia and Egypt and Algeria is that at independence Egypt and Algeria chose to have socialist-like frameworks, whereas in Tunisia, Habib

Lilia Labidi

Bourguiba chose the liberal way for the family and the rights of women.[2]

I think Bourguiba's decision was strongly influenced by the women he met in Tunisia during the struggle against colonialism between the 1930s and 1950s. He was also interested in humanism. Through his lectures and references, we know that he was looking at how we can be attentive to the condition of the whole society. And he did something that was exceptional, because he promulgated the code for women before the constitution was written.

GS: What has been the practical result of all this? How active are women at the professional level?

Labidi: Thirty percent of Tunisian judges are women; more than 33 percent of doctors are women. Roughly half of all university teachers are women. That's not to say that women are strongly represented at every professional level, but they are certainly represented in the public space.

GS: The question, then, is why this happened in Tunisia, but not the rest of northern Africa?

Labidi: That's a great question, but we can't judge all these counties the same way. For example, in Algeria, women were very strongly involved in the struggle against colonialism. At the end, though, they were asked to go home. And women in these countries have been silenced until recently, so we're still learning more about everything that took place.

---

2. Tunisia gained its independence from France in 1956 and became a republic the following year. Habib Bourguiba, an independence leader, served as president until 1987, when he was deposed by his prime minister, Zine el-Abidine Ben Ali.

GS: Let me turn to you then, Haleh, to ask what feminism can do to bring about change. How does it happen? Is there any one way that it happens?

Esfandiari: To add to what Lilia said, the difference between Morocco, Algeria, and Tunisia was that Tunisia had an enlightened leader in Habib Bourguiba, who was not intimidated and introduced these changes. I believe that's been the success story in Tunisia, and that's what we need in all Islamic countries—especially in the Middle East. Of course, you do also need a grassroots movement and an educated middle class of women who are familiar with women's rights and the necessity for changing the current status. But then, you also need leaders in

Haleh Esfandiari

those countries who are not scared to push this agenda.

Let's take some very recent examples, in Kuwait and Bahrain. The emir of Kuwait introduced the possibility of women running and being elected to local councils. In Bahrain, among 300 candidates, 30 were women. Not a single one of them got elected, but at least the women were on the books for the voting. This is an important first step.

Tohidi: I'd like to add to Haleh's comments that in countries such as Iran or most of the rest of the Middle East, the process of modernization, secularization, and reform has been very state-centered. These countries have generally been run in a rather forceful way by authoritarian leaders. That has hindered these movements, since these regimes leave little open space for grassroots women's movements to build. Rights and opportunities for women are usually given to them from the top down. Although some women have been involved in handing down these rights, if there is a backlash in society, the way it happened in Iran, women can easily lose the rights that were gained, because they did not arise from a mass grassroots movement.

Esfandiari: I would beg to disagree with my friend and colleague, Nayereh. With Iran, had we not had the family protection law instituted before the revolution—which gave women the right to seek a divorce, gave child custody to women, gave the right of employment to women, and made polygamy very difficult—I don't think that we would have the few rights that women in Iran have today. I'm very serious about that, because although the family protection law in Iran was suspended immediately after the revolution, those changes had seeped down to the masses of Iranian women, who in turn brought pressure on the government to reintroduce some of those protections. I think the case of Iran shows how those changes had really seeped down.

Labidi: I would add that in the case of Tunisia, when we were independent in 1956, most of the population was illiterate. Now that the relationship between Islam and law has been reformulated to include women, it is the case that the state can be strong. Because even if we had an elite class which was great, and even if we had a group of feminists who were strong, if we didn't have a state which had made a decision to change the code, we would probably be like many other countries. To understand the condition of women, we have to look at the elite and the state.

GS: It seems as though a lot of this has to do with modernity and the fact that populations are now literate and better educated.

Tohidi: One important dimension of modernity is democracy. You can't have a modern society without democracy. One problem with the process of modernization in countries such as Iran and Iraq, and even with the Soviet-style of modernization, has been that it has been very state-centered. It has just been one small, Westernized, modernized elite that has tried to do everything for the rest of society without giving them agencies for participation. There's been little chance for the diversity, the different voices, of women. Everything was in one single organization of women, supported by a state, and everybody had to join that organization. The state is important and must support the women's movement, but there must be roots in civil society and strong women's nongovernmental organizations. The state and the civil society movements must complement each other.

If there's no grassroots movement of women who have struggled for their rights and gained it by their own fight, then they are not going to value it. Turning to Iran again—when the Islamist government nullified the family protection law, there wasn't much resistance because so many people didn't even know about this law.

GS: Nayereh, when you explain it that way, I see that it's everybody's fight, really. To what degree, in any of the countries we're talking about, are women's movements meeting with support from potential male allies? I'm thinking of the intellectual community—universities, journalists, politicians. Does that happen?

Tohidi: I think we'd all agree that there's a great need to reeducate men and bring them into this struggle. They need to be reeducated both at home and in school by changing the curriculum and even the structure of the education system, which is still led in many societies by men, and the texts that perpetuate stereotypical images of womanhood and manhood. Without men's support, as with Bourguiba in Tunisia, for example, women cannot get it done by themselves.

GS: To conclude our conversation, I'd like each of you to make a brief statement about what's most needed for the future advancement of women's rights in Islamic societies.

Tohidi: The biggest problem in the whole Muslim world today is gross underdevelopment—economic, political, social, and cultural. There's also a vigorous fight and debate between the modernist, secularist sector and the religious sector. We must remember that secularism is not necessarily equal to egalitarianism. There are secular people who are very patriarchal, and there are some moderate religious Islamic people who are for equal rights. We are at the verge of a very important struggle between modern forces for change, equality, and democracy and the traditional, conservative, patriarchal forces that are anti-modern, anti-change, and anti-Western. This fight must receive help from the outside, but it must be fought inside by both men and women. Hopefully, the process of globalization will help facilitate reform.

Esfandiari: I'd agree with everything Nayereh said, but I would add that today we basically just talked about the Middle East. The Islamic world goes all the way from Indonesia to Nigeria. But I would like to finish on an optimistic note for the Middle East, because I think that women in the region have started the struggle. They are on the right path, and what we are going to see in the next ten years is an expansion of women's access to education, political participation, and leadership positions.

Labidi: I would like to note that I think in the increasingly globalized twenty-first century, the ideas of Westernized elites and local elites will become less and less important. I also think that the struggle for rights must include a struggle against poverty, as well as the expansion of women's participation from the public square into the political arena.

Originally broadcast June 5, 2002.

7

Joaquim Chissano
A Culture of Peace for Mozambique and Beyond

My interview with the former president of Mozambique was one of the first for dialogue TV, and I remember being shocked by how candid he was. I wasn't used to encountering that level of honesty from any politician, much less from someone who had run a country. I was also impressed that he managed to remain so optimistic and forward thinking, despite being mired in such a terribly bleak situation. Joaquim Chissano stood out as an inspiring example of leadership and continues to do so today. He currently works in Uganda, helping to resolve the brutal twenty-year rebellion of the Lord's Resistance Army.

George Seay: You made a remarkable speech in September of 2000 before the United Nations, and in that speech you said something that I very much want to ask you about. You very poetically said, "Humanity itself is a civilization." That's a wonderful phrase. What did you mean by it?

Chissano: The theme of the meeting was dialogue among civilizations, and I meant that it was difficult for me to divide the world into different civilizations in my mind. I get lost.

Let's take the example of Mozambique. We have adopted Portuguese as the official language of the country. We have numerous cultures. We take habits and customs from India, from the Arab world, and from the Swahili world. So you find the world is actually very small.

GS: You have given the world many great messages on many different questions, including aspects of globalization that we in America or Europe perhaps don't think that much about. For example, has it been your concern that the process of globalization and economic trade may be, to some extent, marginalizing certain countries?

Chissano: Yes, indeed. The concept of globalization has always been one of marginalizing, as in the past we had globalizers, and it was the people who were globalized. I'm speaking about the time when we had slavery, of course.

People were exploited, and thus excluded. So globalization has been characterized by exclusion for a long time. We have now arrived at a time when we think globalization is inevitable. It's here. What we need is to correct it. Building on this concept of being one culture and one humanity, we should remember that those who gain from globalization will start losing themselves if they continue to exclude others. Globalization must be based on equality and democracy and participation of people in the construction of the world, so that all can enjoy the benefits of this construction.

I think that this is being understood today because people are starting to speak more and more in terms of partnerships instead of donors and recipients. People speak about partnership for mutual benefits, instead of speaking of charity alone. The wealthy and developed countries are starting to understand that when they give, they also receive something.

And they also know that if they ask for reciprocity from someone who has nothing to reciprocate, they will get the worst. They may get migration, terrorism, drug trafficking, and the other things that come with leaving poor people behind. AIDS will spread everywhere, and then the world will be in a mess. So, the losers will be those who had something, because those who had nothing, had nothing to lose.

GS: You are a statesman, sir, not simply of Africa, but of the world, and I think one of the reasons that I'm absolutely certain that you hold that high place is because you have done so much for the cause of peace.

Violence is a problem everywhere, as we both know. And in your own history there was the war for independence from Portugal, which lasted a long time and was very costly. There was a great deal of civil conflict after what Mozambique had to suffer through. But in building peace, you talk about something you called "the culture of peace." What exactly is the culture of peace? What are its values? How do you make peace happen?

Chissano: The culture of peace is that part of the culture—it's not different from culture—which upholds the ideals of equality and fraternity among the peoples. It is based on the ability to search for forgiveness and tolerance, because we have conflicts from the family point of view, and from the community point of view. And the only way of living in harmony in a family is that you have ways of sitting and discussing the differences. You accept the differences, you discuss them, and you find a solution. And when you're hurt, you have to find ways to forgive and try to participate in such a way that the wrong things are not repeated by the other members of the family.

GS: Are you saying, President Chissano, that the nation ideally should see itself as a family? That the same need for forgiveness and dialogue is needed in society as it is in family?

Chissano: Yes, because in the family, you recognize first the idea that you are members of that family and you want that family to be great. In a nation, you must agree that this is our nation and we want it to be great, and that our differences are nothing compared to what we want to achieve as a nation. So, we must achieve a common understanding. That's why in Mozambique we are busy discussing within the society at large the vision of the country for the next twenty-five years.

GS: In addition to building and preserving peace, you have also made very strong statements about democracy and the importance of democracy to Mozambique and so many other countries. You've been president now for two terms and you have already said that you are not going to run in 2004. Succession in a democracy, most will agree, is vital. Is that one of the reasons that you are saying you're going to step down and not run again?

Chissano: The main reason, actually, is a moral reason. It has to do with myself, because then I may say that I never went to look for power, and this is my only chance to demonstrate that. According to the constitution, I could still run again. The economy is going well, so I'm not running from difficulties. People are applauding me now. So, it's the best time to go and to demonstrate that we are not there to be there forever. We can be replaced.

GS: Let me ask you about a very important aspect of what you and Mozambique are concerned with right now—regional security and peace. Peace in Africa, beyond just Mozambique. I know that, at the moment, you chair the security committee of the Southern African Development Committee.[1]

This seems to me to be a crucial moment for the question of peace in Africa. Jonas Savimbi recently died in Angola, and there are many questions about what that will mean. Peace talks in Congo are just now beginning. There's a very tense situation in Zimbabwe and other places. Putting all that together, what kind of moment is this for peace in Africa? Is it a fragile moment, a dangerous moment, or both?

Chissano: I think we have more hopes than one may think. We had a hard time getting the Congolese to sit down and have discussions. This must give us hope. The difficulties during dialogue are not a problem. Those will be there, but must be overcome.

In Mozambique, it took us two years of direct dialogue between the two sides after some years of preparation. These talks required a lot of patience, a sense of tolerance, and perseverance. So I think that in the Congo, if they have this perseverance, they will get there. But what is needed more immediately is that the world comes to help them come together, and doesn't try to divide them by trying to favor negotiations according to interests of each country. In the past, this has complicated the search for peace and the resolution of conflicts.

And in Angola, Savimbi was one of the major elements—perhaps the greatest element—against peace and stability. Now he is dead. It's unfortunate that he is dead, and I never cheer the death of anyone, but he could have avoided this kind of death. But it's one obstacle which is removed and there are chances for progress in the search for peace.

GS: You mentioned a moment ago that the world has to come to the aid of Congo to help it, rather than divide it. And perhaps

---

1. Chissano completed his term in February 2005.

the same thing is true of the AIDS crisis. What should the world be doing to confront the growing problem of AIDS?

Chissano: I think the world should be more generous in bringing assistance for all the programs which have been designed in different countries to combat AIDS. In our region, for instance, Botswana has a very good program, and Mozambique has a very good program. What we need are means for us to move quickly and contact whole populations. We are working in the schools, and we need to be more active, and we need to have means for prevention.

We have started training personnel in order to make use of anti-retroviral medicines and to establish centers to monitor the disease and stop it wherever it may be stopped. But we will need means after the training. The training process itself requires lots of means. And then, of course, you need the medicines, and the medicines are expensive. So while the research for vaccines is going on, the medicines must be made available.

Originally broadcast March 20, 2002.

8

Jared Diamond
The Shaping of Human Societies

Among academics, a select few manage to bring their work into the mainstream of societal discussion. Jared Diamond is one of those. A professor of geology and, until recently, physiology at UCLA, his scholarship is rooted in the specialized study of physiology, membrane biophysics, the ecology of New Guinea birds, and environmental history, but his popular books tackle the widest aspects of history. His Pulitzer Prize-winning Guns, Germs, and Steel: The Fates of Human Societies, *explores human development on the basis of geography and environment.[1]*

※

George Seay: Iraq is in very troubled circumstances these days, eight thousand years after its dominant position in the world. Jared, explain through the context of your book why this has happened and what lessons it has for us.

Diamond: The book is about differences among people in the modern world. There are rich, technologically advantaged people, and there are poor people. And a common interpretation, almost a transparent interpretation, is that rich people are rich because

---

1. Jared Diamond, *Guns, Germs, and Steel: The Fates of Human Societies* (Norton, 1997).

they're smart and they work hard, and poor people are poor because they're dumb and they don't work hard.

For example, the argument would go that Europeans are smarter and Aboriginal Australians are hunter-gatherers because they are less smart. The fact is that it takes an awful lot of brains to eek out a living in the Australian desert.

And the other fact is that if you look at what has happened over the last twelve thousand years, Eurasian societies got ahead because of some strokes of bio-geographic luck. Namely, they were in the areas where there were more wild plants and animals that could be domesticated. Most plants and animals can't be, but wheat, cattle, sheep, and pigs can. In the United States, oak trees and deer could not be domesticated, so Eurasian people got a head start on farming, which meant villages, which meant settled living, technology, states, and so on. That's the argument of the book.

Then comes your interesting question about Iraq. Iraq led the world ten thousand years ago. Iraq was where agriculture rose. It was where the first writing system developed. It was the site of the first state and the first metal tools. Why did the society that led the world end up as a basket case today, except for its oil?

The answer is what could be called ecological suicide. Namely, that the fertile crescent is an environmentally fragile area of low rainfall, and so, when you cut down trees, they grow back slowly. When you cut down trees in South Carolina or New Guinea, they grow back quickly. The result is that Iraq and the so-called fertile crescent, where agriculture began, got deforested and the salt came up to the surface of the soil, destroying what had been the oldest farm lands in the world.

The result is that, gradually, over the last ten thousand years, Iraq, Iran, Jordan, Syria, and southeastern Turkey—the center of civilization—lost their natural advantages.

GS: Is there a lesson in that for us during this so-called super-power moment we are experiencing?

Diamond: Absolutely, as we in the United States and many of the countries in the world are facing environmental problems of forest, water, and salt—problems that dragged down Iraq and the Maya civilization, as well as many other societies.

GS: The central question of this book seems to be, "Why do certain societies have so much, while others have so little?" To begin with, you make a very strong point throughout the book of emphatically rejecting notions of biological racial superiority.

You write that, "History followed different courses for different peoples because of differences among people's environments, not because of biological differences among people themselves."

That's a very powerful point that you make repeatedly. Why do you feel so strongly about it?

Diamond: I feel strongly about it simply because it's correct and not because of any starting assumption. For one, despite all the efforts of racist psychologists and statisticians over the past century to try to find evidence that Europeans or Chinese are smarter than New Guineans or Native Americans, they haven't come up with any evidence.

And second, in my own experience working in the tropical island of New Guinea, north of Australia, where until recently people were using stone tools and had very little in the way of clothing—so-called primitive people—I naively expected to find that they were primitive and would be mentally backwards. But it took me about a day to realize that these are really smart people. In fact, it gradually dawned on me that on average, they're at least as smart—probably smarter—than Americans and Europeans and Japanese whom I've had as friends and dealt with.

And so the question gradually forced itself on me: Why is it that these smart people ended up with the stone tools, without writing, while I the dope, who still can't light a fire in the jungle when it's raining, arrive there as a representative of the metal tool-using culture, with writing? And it was that question that led me to get into the research for the book, which made me realize that it was the result of ten thousand years of history and environments.

GS: Essential to reading and understanding this book is your point about what you call proximate and ultimate causes. Let's see if I got it right. If I were to say that the British created their empire because they had ships and guns and the wherewithal technologically and strategically to do it, I would be identifying the proximate cause of what happened. But as you explain it, the ultimate cause would come from the answer to the question of what led them to have the "guns, germs, and steel" to pull that off?

Diamond: That's a good example of proximate and ultimate causes. Let's take a more familiar example. Suppose the following: A man comes to me in the morning and says, "I'm suing for divorce because my wife slapped me in the face."

That's the proximate clause for his suing for divorce. But then I ask him, "Why did your wife slap you in the face?" He replies, "Oh, I've been having affairs for years and gambling and spending down the money."

The ultimate cause of the divorce is that he is having affairs and spending down the money. The proximate clause of his divorce is her slapping him in the face.

GS: You talk about the point where the Aboriginal people of Australia actually went to Australia via the sea. They use what you call water craft to get there, and they are sailing from a point they obviously know to one they don't know, crossing an uncharted ocean to invisible islands, as you call them.

Diamond: The ancestors of Aboriginal Australians set out in a "great leap forward." Australia, as far as we can tell, was reached by humans for the first time about 46,000 years ago. Australia is separated by water gaps from Southeast Asia, where there had been humans, but to get to Australia required water craft. They might have been simple light rafts—they didn't have to be sailing canoes—but it still required going over water.

And there's the question, as you say: why would people sitting on the Indonesian island of Timor, 120 miles away, set out for an island, Australia, that they couldn't even see? There are a couple of possibilities. One is that they didn't set out. They were fishing and a wind came up and they were blown away and most of them drowned. But eventually, a raft with one pregnant woman on it washed up on the coast of Australia and she bore a son, and that was the origins of the Aboriginal Australians.

The other possibility is that they did it intentionally. There they were on the coast of Timor and they look out to sea and see birds and stars and other things, and they keep seeing in that direction that there seems to be haze or smoke. Now, they know in Timor in the dry season there are fires, and they figure out that smoke means fires. In Timor, the resources are getting depleted and some young man who's pretty desperate says, "I'm sure those fires mean there's a big land and I'm going to become rich and famous and so if you young women will join me, we'll have all those hunting grounds." They set off, and again most of them drown, but one raft arrives. Those are the two possibilities.

GS: That brings me to the role of farming. I worked on a farm as a kid, and from reading this book, it's clear that the farmer is absolutely pivotal, the linchpin of what happens. Because this is what moves us from hunter-gatherers to settled agriculture and creates surpluses that, in turn, allow societies to become more complex. What's your comment on the role of the farmer?

Diamond: The farmer is indeed the linchpin, because in order to have metal tools and writing and empires, you need to be settled down in villages. And you need to have food surpluses that can feed these kings and these intellectuals who are sitting down in the village and thinking out how to devise a writing system, and figuring out how to smelt metal. Those things did not arise in nomadic hunter-gatherer societies that can't accumulate food surpluses.

The possibility of food surpluses arose for the first time in human history with farming, where you could then grow wheat and you had one farmer who could grow two, to five, to a hundred times more wheat than he or she needed for himself or herself, and his or her family. All that surplus food can be stored, and then can be used to feed these characters who don't go out and hunt goats or elephants, or till the fields, but instead sit down in the village. The kings give orders, but they're also playing around with materials, and they stumble across smelting, and they scratch and they come onto writing systems. So farming was required for two things: sedentary living and food surpluses, from which everything interesting flows.

GS: I want to turn now to my favorite chapter, "Collision at Cajamarca," which describes the encounter between around 600 troops under the command of the Spaniard Francisco Pizarro and roughly 80,000 Incas and their emperor, Atahuallpa. The Spaniards defeat, and essentially slaughter, the Incas using deceit, horses, and, of course, guns and strategy. The steel here was in their swords, and they benefited from the fact that germs had been spread earlier—an epidemic of smallpox that decimated the Incan forces.

I'd love for you to comment on that because it seemed to me

that this story was emblematic of this whole notion of conquest of a complex society over one that is in a different status.

Diamond: If you could give me a time machine that would allow me to dial a place and time and I could get just one dial, I think I would dial Cajamarca in 1532. It was even more dramatic because Pizarro did not have 600 Spaniards; he had only 169 Spaniards. He was there, lost in the middle of the most powerful empire of the New World, the Inca Empire, and there facing him was the Inca army of 80,000 under the command of its emperor, Atahuallpa. When the Spaniards arrived there and looked out at night and saw these thousands and thousands of camp fires burning, they were so terrified that one of them wrote, "We were urinating in our trousers we were so scared."

And yet, the next morning, when Atahuallpa and his bearers, 6,000 of them, came up to the Spanish camp, within about ten minutes the battle was all over. The Spaniards fired off some guns which didn't kill anybody, but made a loud sound and scared the Incas, who had never faced guns. And then out came the horses, which the Incas had also never encountered.

The Spaniards charged the Incas on their horses using steel swords, cut down most of Atahuallpa's bodyguard force of 6,000, captured the emperor himself, then rode out into the fields and began killing Incas in the fields. By the end of the day, there were between 6,000 and 9,000 Incas dead, and the Spaniards held the emperor of the most powerful state of the New World captive. They held him captive for months, extracted a ransom, and took over the empire.

GS: The battle itself, as I recall, was set off when Atahuallpa disdainfully tossed a Bible to the ground, which caused a priest at the head of Pizarro's forces to become outraged and call for the—well, what they were going to do anyway—to start this battle. The battle commenced soon thereafter.

What is the role of religion in all this? You say that certain religions historically have proselytized and used force. You made the argument that conquest was a very powerful motive in many of the great religions.

Diamond: Religion certainly has furnished a powerful motive, and I would say that it's an open question as to whether religion is simply an excuse, or whether it's an independent force. That is to say, when one people conquers and kills another people, usually they need to tell themselves something for why it is justified, because some part of us says that it's not nice to kill other people.

If we can do it exceptionally, we need justification, and often that justification has been religion—that we have the right religion, that those people are infidels and have the wrong religion. In the Bible, in the book of Joshua, Joshua slaughters 600 villagers and kills everybody, and it's okay because he's got the right religion and they've got the wrong religion. So religion has often been used as the excuse for states that had the guns, germs, and steel to wipe out other people.

GS: How do you feel when you hear commentators or critics refer to your book's arguments as geographic determinism?

Diamond: It's disagreeable. And commentators who say that the book is geographic determinism in general have not read it but have heard about it from somebody else. In fact, the book is about geographic factors that influence the development of human society. But when we hear geographic determinism, we react to it negatively. We think that it means that humans are forced to do a certain thing, there is no free will, and we are pawns of the environment. But it's not true.

The fact that you and I are talking today is the result of human genius and inventiveness over the last 50,000 years. It's simply that some environments provide more starting materials than other environments, which made it easier for people to invent and to come up with things. But it doesn't mean that everything was predetermined in great detail.

GS: Thinking further ahead, what might be the policy implications of this story of the haves and have-nots? What can and should be done, in terms of bridging the gap between those who have and those who do not have, and particularly the responsibility of a nation as rich as this one?

Diamond: Perhaps the most direct policy implications are that if one people, or one segment of society, has less money than another segment of society, it doesn't mean that they're dumb and should be written off and not provided with opportunities for education. Rather, it's been a matter of opportunities.

And a practical example of that is when the United States sixty-five years ago looked down on people in Eastern Asia and Southeast Asia, using various unpleasant pejorative terms, and regarded East Asians as inferior—and then we were very surprised at Pearl Harbor to find that torpedoes that operated in shallow water like no European torpedoes were able to sink eight of our battleships in a very short time. And it took us four-and-a-half years, despite enormous material advantages, to end that war. It was an enormous mistake, and it was a mistake on our part that resulted from our racist disparagement of other people.

The message is that it is dangerous to dismiss other people on the grounds of a supposed lack of intelligence, because if you do, then you may be very surprised. And in the modern world, since September 11th, we've discovered that people anywhere, even in some remote, landlocked country like Afghanistan, have the potential for causing us lots of trouble.

GS: In that context, you advocate—not just in this book, but in other writings—the idea of crisis prevention—trying to do something in troubled countries about poverty, illiteracy, bad health care, and so forth—to prevent the kinds of bad outcomes that we often see. In that sense, it's a very pragmatic security matter.

Diamond: Just to put numbers on it: the Afghanistan intervention and the Iraq intervention alone cost something like $80 or $100 billion each, and that's not even talking about all the money for the subsequent buildup. In contrast, the amount of money it would take to get well-launched on curing AIDS and malaria and tuberculosis is estimated at about $25 billion, one-quarter of an Iraq-Afghanistan intervention. If you could get rid of those three major public health problems of the world, then you would have solved ultimate causes and you wouldn't have to put in $100 billion every time some country like Somalia or Afghanistan blows up.

Originally broadcast March 22, 2004.

9

George Kennan

Rebuilding Trust between Russia and the United States

George F. Kennan, diplomat, political scientist, and historian, and I crossed paths three times. First, I was his student at Princeton in a small foreign policy seminar he taught from his home. Then, he helped found and shape the Wilson Center's Kennan Institute—named not for himself but for a nineteenth-century relative, an explorer of Russia—and so was a frequent visitor. Third, was this opportunity to talk with him in the studio. What surprised me most was that, despite his reputation for detachment among some critics, he was vitally concerned with American society and culture. George Kennan died March 17, 2005.

George Seay: What can you tell us about the current state of U.S.-Russian relations?

Kennan: I think we ought to make every effort to meet the Russians on the academic and cultural plane, even though there are great problems, questions, and difficulties on the political level. On the political level, it's just going to take patience.

There's one thing I have tried to tell people when they've asked me to talk about Russia today and that is they must bear in mind that this is a deeply injured country. This last century has dealt very brutally with Russia, starting with the Russian-Japanese War. The enormous manpower losses of the First World War; the Revolution and all the destruction of the old intelligentsia; Stalin and his purges. And then the Second World War and tremendous manpower losses again.

As all of us who have lived in that country know, all of these things have drained Russia of a great deal of its promise.

I can remember when I left there. The last time I served was in 1952, and I went out in the countryside to try to find out what was happening in the villages. We found that the fields and the entire farming process were being left to old women and children. The men had been drained out of the village for military service and the great bureaucratic apparatus of the Communist party.

Socially, this has been a deeply injured country. The family structure of an orderly civilization, where a man could grow up in or near the household of his parents and families could be kept together, ceased to exist. All of that was destroyed in Russia, and this country almost has to start from the beginning again. I think it's going to take another generation before it becomes anywhere near normal.

GS: I cannot resist asking about the "X" article and your intentions when you wrote that, because as we all know, that was a document of extraordinary importance to American foreign policy and it set off, in its wake, a concept of containment that may not have been the one you sought.[1]

Kennan: That is true, and I was to blame for it. In November or December of 1946, just before General George Marshall appeared on the scene and asked me to set up the policy planning staff

---

1. "X" [George F. Kennan], "The Sources of Soviet Conduct," *Foreign Affairs* (July 1947).

and to give him an opinion of what he should do about Europe, the editor of *Foreign Affairs,* Ham Armstrong, asked me to attend a dinner at the Council on Foreign Relations to talk about Russia as I had seen it and the United States' relationship to it. Which I did.

Afterward, Armstrong asked me if I had my comments in the talk written out anywhere, and I told him that I didn't think I really had, but that I'd go back and look at my papers, and perhaps I could give him the gist of it. I ended up just sitting down at Christmastime, a very busy time, and I pounded the article out on the typewriter there in the old War College building and sent it off to Armstrong.

I made the great mistake of not realizing that people would not understand that there could be containment that was not of a military nature. There were military aspects to it, certainly, but I also had in mind the efforts the Russians were making to penetrate other countries—not just the proletariat, but also the intellectuals. They were having a certain success with this in England, in France, in Italy, and, of course, in Germany, where there was still great uncertainty and people didn't know what to think.

GS: The language is typically eloquent. In one passage, you advocate "the adroit and vigilant application of counterforce to meet Soviet expansionism." Yet you didn't mean just militarily.

Kennan: No, I meant counterpressure. I had in mind that where they were, for example, penetrating academic student organizations—quite successfully in some instances—we had to really

oppose that. There were some who agreed with me that we had to really meet them on the intellectual level. But that statement was much too cryptic and lent itself to misinterpretation.

GS: That misinterpretation manifested itself in part in the creation of NATO, which has now been around for fifty years. It has expanded and is now currently active in the Balkans. What are your views on that as NATO's boundaries, so to speak, have come closer to Russia. Has that been a cause for concern for you?

Kennan: As you may know from my memoirs, I never saw a proper reason for setting up NATO. That was not the problem at that time, so I've always had a certain skepticism about it. There have been a great many people that I've respected and admired connected with NATO, so I don't want to carry it too far, but I think it's regrettable that an institution which aspired to be the unifying institution for all of Europe should have been, by its own dedication and charter, a military one, rather than a non-military one.

I think that Europe's problems were much deeper than just military ones, and particularly after the breakdown of the Soviet government, I was unable to understand, and didn't approve of, the expansion of NATO into Eastern Europe. Nobody was threatening anybody at that time. The idea that the Russians were going to invade any of these countries was flawed.

People remembered the past, but they forgot a great deal about the past, too. They don't remember that what brought Stalin's power into Eastern Europe was really the pursuit of Hitler and the invasion of German forces into the center of Europe, and we wouldn't have wanted it to be otherwise. We welcomed the advance of the Red Army at that time.

The only thing we didn't know was how to get them out, once they had gotten in. That was all very bad, but the answer was not fully a military one and shouldn't have been seen that way. So I have never been very happy about this and the extension of

NATO's boundaries to Eastern Europe. I thought there could have been other ways of relieving the anxieties of the Poles, Hungarians, and Czechs. There were other ways that would have been less provocative to the Russians and lent themselves less to misunderstanding.

Originally broadcast February 14, 2000.

PART II

American Leaders, Prophets, and Critics

10

Gen. Benjamin O. Davis Jr.

A Tuskegee Airman on Service, Leadership, and Tenacity

My conversation with Benjamin Davis, leader of the famed Tuskegee Airmen of World War II, remains the only interview I've done that literally produced goose bumps the minute the man walked into the studio. He had that archetypical gentleman's look—full head of white hair, carefully groomed and brushed back, ramrod straight posture, controlled yet decisive gestures. Davis confronted racism and discrimination throughout his life, but consistently rose above it, becoming the U.S. Air Force's first African American general. Courageous, principled, and dignified, he leaves us with an inspirational legacy of leadership and integrity. Benjamin Davis died July 4, 2002.

George Seay: General, as I read your book, one of the first thoughts that occurred to me is that in reading biography, one of the pleasures the reader has is acting as a kind of detective.[1]

[1] Benjamin O. Davis, *Benjamin O. Davis Jr., American: An Autobiography* (Smithsonian, 1991).

We're constantly searching for those incidents and events that form the character of the individual and set the themes in the life that comes after.

I want to talk with you about one of the stories that made a great impression on me. It takes place on a hot summer night in Alabama. You call it "the night of the Klan" in the book, and a pivotal figure is your father, Brigadier General Davis, who was on the staff of the Tuskegee Institute at that time. To summarize the story, the staff, students, and faculty had been warned that the Klan was going to march that night. Everyone is recommended to be in hiding, houses should be darkened, and most of the people do exactly that. Practically all save for one—your father, who makes a very different decision.

He has his family dressed and sitting on the porch, right there under the porch light, and he is sitting there himself in his Army dress whites as a reproach to the Ku Klux Klan. So it's a very powerful scene when you read it. And I'm wondering how it affected you, both then when you were a boy and then later in life.

Davis: Believe it or not, this is seventy years later and I can see it this very minute as we sit here in downtown Washington, D.C. In the first place, I had heard of the Klan. I was about eight or nine years old at that time. And I knew about the Klan just in general terms, but I was very confused about the fact that some hostile strangers would invade our territory in their robes, their hoods, their flaming torches, in an attempt, as I learned later, to intimidate people. I was impressed by the fact that my father was not going to be intimidated. He felt that as a regular Army officer, he should not cower from the Klan.

GS: And he did not.

Davis: He did not, as you pointed out. He had on his white dress uniform, and I sat with him, my mother, and my two sisters on that porch with the porch light above us.

GS: That answer brings out several themes—pride, courage, defiance—themes that are also going to be important in your own life as you continue to develop your career later on.

In light of that, I want to ask you this key question, because one of the most riveting and wrenching chapters in your entire book is the episode at West Point and your four years there. I think many readers would do as I did when I read that chapter. I actually went back and read it twice.

Here we have a young man who has chosen a military career and has been selected to enter West Point in 1932, to graduate in 1936. And you are subjected to four years of silencing, which means that none of your peers are going to speak with you, or even choose to eat with you if they can get out of it. This is very well documented in the book. How does a man, one who has just barely passed adolescence, endure that?

Davis: I was still very young and foolish and idealistic. I believed in duty, honor, and country, for one thing. Believe it or not, I really believed in it. Deeply did I believe in it. Another thing is that I wanted to fly airplanes, and I believed very strongly that if I graduated from West Point, the Army Air Corps couldn't turn me down. Well, I was very wrong about that, as you found out, too. Very wrong.

But I didn't ever abandon the goal of graduating from West Point in the hope that I would be accepted by the Army Air Corps, and it wasn't until I was turned down in the fall of 1935, in my last year at West Point, that I realized that I was not going to be able to fly.

GS: That's right. What you did is very real and very moving to me. Let me ask you this point blank. I am deeply disturbed about the sheepish attitude, if you will, of your peers who sort of adopted this silencing attitude unthinkingly, in many cases. I suspect that it might have been a situation in which there were ringleaders guiding the whole group's behavior. Do you have any thoughts about that?

Davis: I certainly do. There is a very clear statement in that book—a quote from the commandant of cadets, Lieutenant Colonel Robert C. Richardson, who made the statement to me personally that cadets are like sheep and they were the followers of, as you mentioned just now, a few ringleaders who dominated the scene.

And as a matter of fact, one of my classmates related to another person recently, about a month ago, that he was just a young, skinny boy from Mississippi and he didn't approve of what was happening to me at that time. But he knew in his heart that if he raised any protest about it, he would never have gotten through West Point. That particular individual rose to the rank of major general, United States Army.

GS: In spite of all that, though, you did triumph at West Point. Graduation was triumph. And your wish to fly, just to put this in perspective, was nothing more than an act of faith because the Army was not about to allow that. In 1925, the Army had published its own study concluding that blacks weren't fit for flying. But it did happen. It happened in a very dramatic way. How in fact did that come about?

Davis: Well, there was a lot of pressure put on the Army and those pressures resulted in a directive on the part of the president to the War Department to train blacks for the Army Air Corps, and that really was the beginning of the 99th Pursuit Squadron, which changed the face of the Armed Forces permanently. It was the 99th Pursuit Squadron and the follow-on squadrons of the 332nd Fighter Group that set the stage for integration of the Armed Forces.

GS: Let's talk about the 99th and the 332nd, which brings us back to Tuskegee, where our story started. One of the ironies is that the Tuskegee Army Air Field, where the 99th, an all-black fighter squadron, was trained, was itself a bastion of segregation. It's just that simple.

When I try to even imagine those times, I'm trying to get a sense of how hundreds of well-motivated young men, undergoing this arduous training, could really cope with a situation like that. It must have been terribly frustrating to live with it on the base, as well as in the society.

Davis: George, it was the influence of the airplane. Most of these young men had been fighting for the previous six, seven years trying to fly airplanes. I had been one of them. We put up with all sorts of foolishness and denigration in order to fly airplanes and demonstrate that, yes, black people could fly airplanes. We knew we could fly, but they didn't think we could, and that was ridiculous.

GS: General, when you took the 99th and the 332nd into action in North Africa and Europe, you compiled an astounding record. There's no other way to put it. It was a record of extraordinary distinction.

I want to hear you talk about that record, but also about something that you, as a commanding officer, were particularly concerned with—what I call the backstage battle. I got the impression that there were two distinct battles going on. One was the fight to prove supremacy in the air, which the 99th and 332nd won dramatically. But the other was a backstage battle with people submitting memoranda and questioning how the group was performing, in some cases by outright lying. Now you, more than your men, were dealing with this second battle. Tell us about that.

Davis: This was probably the most difficult part of my service in the military, without question. A memorandum was submitted by the Mediterranean Theater of Operation which very clearly recommended that the 99th Pursuit Squadron be removed from combat because they showed a tendency to break up in combat. It said that the squadron showed a lack of discipline in the air and other similar charges.

I don't know whether that memo truly originated in the theater or whether the people in the theater were told to submit such a report, so that blacks could be relegated to the rather sterile job of coastal patrol.

But when I went back to take command of the 332nd Fighter Group, they had me appear before the McCloy Committee at the Pentagon in the middle of October of 1943. I was just about as mad as I've ever been in my entire life. But I felt that I had to handle this thing very carefully. I think it would have been fatal to cry racism. Instead, very quietly, coolly, and dispassionately, I told the story of the 99th, and the fact that they were eager to defend their country and fly airplanes in spite of the background that had existed at Tuskegee Army Air Field.

And evidently somebody listened. I think it was probably George Marshall, the secretary of war. What he did was to direct the creation of a study by G-3 Operations of the War Department. And that did the trick. The study showed beyond any doubt whatsoever that the 99th was equal to the other five P-40 squadrons in the theater, if not superior. I read the statistics and I've got a copy of that report at home to this day. And I read the statistics to show that the 99th was superior.

GS: It was an extraordinary record. Just to cite one aspect of it that I know about—your Red Tails were assigned bomber escort and never lost a bomber.

Davis: Yes, and I must mention to you, for the first time ever on the air, a letter I received dated June 5, 1991, from a pilot of the Fifth Wing B-17 outfit. He tells the story of a combat mission in which he had dropped back behind the formation in order to take a look at another B-17. He saw behind him the Red Tails of the 332nd as well as five Messerschmitts as they dove on the B-17. He observed the Red Tail pilots destroy all five of the Messerschmitts as they dove on that B-17.

And at the end of the letter he said, "General, I went over to your group base after this mission. We wanted to thank you. You were away flying, and only three of your pilots did we see. We were never able to go back. But I want to tell you in this letter that I thank you for the lives of my crew and for the members of the other airplane that these five Messerschmitts were attacking. Without your action, all of our lives would have been lost."

GS: The years of 1947–48 were an extraordinary chapter in American history. How do you look back on that period now and assess its importance to society, because I think the Armed Forces integration, together with *Brown v. Board of Education* in 1954, were the pillars for what happened in civilian society over the next decades.

Davis: I agree completely. And as a matter of fact, it is without question the proudest part of my service. It was a great time for us. I'll never forget the time when President Harry Truman issued his Executive Order 9981—I even remember the number—that mandated equal opportunity and treatment for all people assigned to the Armed Forces of the United States. That was 1948.

And then the leadership of the United States Air Force—Stuart

Symington, the secretary, and Hoyt Vandenberg, the general chief of staff—had confidence in us because of what they had observed black airmen do during World War II. They knew that they had a tremendously great asset in black airmen who would perform well anywhere, whether they were in a white unit or a black unit. And that's why they felt free to send them all over the world.

GS: Hearing you explain it that way, General, it seems to me that your whole life has really been one man's argument for meritocracy and people being treated according to their talents and their abilities, for being treated fairly and equally right across the board.

Now, of course, your life after the active military phase of it really touched upon just about every major concern of American society today—urban affairs, environmental affairs, consumer affairs, terrorism. When you look at the society which you have served so well, what do you think our major problems are right now?

Davis: In my mind, the number one problem is racism and personal relationships of Americans to one another. And unfortunately, it still exists in the Armed Forces a little bit, too, because there are people who have not been properly brought up by their parents. You have moms and pops who teach their children that the little black person next door—that little nigger next door—is not as good as you. Or that you're far superior to such and such a person because he's a Jew. Or you're far superior to him because he doesn't look the same as you, or he's Hispanic.

This is the problem in America today and it is a problem that will last throughout the remainder of my life. But America has got to come to grips with this problem more effectively.

GS: One of the things that I enjoyed most about your book and that impressed me the most about your life is that through all that's happened, through all you've achieved, I can really see changes in the man through the progression of chapters. And one of the most interesting concerns leadership. What does leadership mean to General Benjamin O. Davis Jr.?

Davis: Leadership first means knowing where you want to go, because if you don't know where you want to go, you can't lead anybody. And once you've decided what is highly moral and desirable to pursue, you've got to convince others with whom you are associated that it is desirable to move in a certain direction and you must convince them that it is to their advantage to participate in an effort that is broad-based. No one can do it alone, and that is my philosophy of what the word *leadership* really means to me.

You've got to work with people and you've got to respect people. You've got to like people. And you cannot fake it. You've got to like the people with whom you work, and they've got to know that you respect them and their capabilities. If they have that type of feeling, they'll go to the ends of the earth for you.

Originally broadcast July 12, 1991.

11

Bill Bradley

Race in America: A Call for "Straight Talk" and Open Dialogue

When I sat down to talk with Bill Bradley about race in America, I was not prepared for how personally the issue moved him. As he described his boyhood in a small town in Missouri, internship on Capitol Hill, and first profession as a star basketball player for the New York Knicks, he demonstrated how closely he had experienced what he was talking about. In recent years, Bradley, a U.S. senator from 1979 to 1996 and a presidential candidate in 2000, has been a teacher and speaker and the author of several books, the latest being The New American Story.[1]

❋

George Seay: It's great to have you here, Senator Bradley. You know, I must say I have been extremely impressed with the number of speeches you've recently made on the subject of race in America. They've occurred in a variety of places—on the floor of the Senate, the National Press Club, and, of course, the Democratic National Convention. Without wishing to be overly flattering, I'd characterize these speeches as both eloquent and tough. But I'd also add a third characterization. They seem to me

---

[1] Bill Bradley, *The New American Story* (Random House, 2007).

very personal. Am I right in that suspicion, and if so, what precisely has motivated your deep interest in the subject?

Bradley: Yes, you are right. They are very personal. In fact, one of the reasons I'm in public life today is because of the issue of race in America. I remember back in 1964, when I was a student intern here in Washington, I was in the Senate chamber on the night that the 1964 Civil Rights Act passed. That bill, of course, desegregated hotels, restaurants, and other public accommodations, among other things. And as I stood in the corner of the Senate chamber that night, watching the votes being counted and seeing it pass, I thought to myself, "You know, something has happened in this chamber tonight that will make America a better place for white Americans, for black Americans—for all Americans."

And it occurred to me at that moment that someday perhaps I could be in the Senate and help to make America a better place. So my definition of making America a better place and the origin of that thought were inextricably related to the issue of race in America and the challenge that our Founders really posed to us in the Declaration: to realize the potential of our ideals.

GS: I find that a striking answer because it suggests two things to me. First, it suggests a very deep sense of personal experience and commitment. But also, there's a sense of our own history as a kind of commandment to make progress on this issue.

Now, you came from a small town in Missouri and your athletic career took you to Princeton and then to professional basketball. You obviously mixed and had close friendships with people of other races and backgrounds.

Bradley: That's certainly true. I played professional basketball for ten years, and that was a predominantly black world. I was moving in a society that was dominantly white, but the team itself was dominantly black, so I had a chance to see the country through the eyes of my teammates and saw it a little differently than I might have seen it had I been traveling on my own. And I think that experience was a very important one for me, and one that I'll never forget. It's seared in my imagination and memory.

The issue of race goes deeper than that, though—much further back than my basketball days—but there is no question that the experience of traveling with an extraordinary group of human beings on the road in America during the 1960s and 1970s was a tremendous experience.

GS: I have heard few other speakers actually address the often unflattering way that people perceive each other. I don't want to be accused of making a bad play on the title of this program, but you seem to be making a call for dialogue.

Bradley: Well, I think that's very true. I think people go through life in separate channels and rarely engage. People are afraid to talk about the reality that's out there, whether that reality is violence or poverty or discrimination. Whatever the reality is, people tread on the truth very, very gingerly. They aren't interested in really getting down to the truth of the issues sometimes, because that means that they have to put themselves on the line, and people aren't willing to do that if they don't have to and the dominant culture doesn't require them to. So people continue to carry certain stereotypes of them, of other races, whatever that race is.

GS: You've often called for "straight talk," and in so doing, you have, in a very bipartisan and general way, been critical of our society for not having candid communication, and critical of the political community for not meeting its full responsibility.

Bradley: I think both Democrats and Republicans are to blame here. There's been a conspiracy of silence on the issue. Republicans have overtly used race to divide people in order to get votes over the last twenty-five years. The Willie Horton ad in 1998 was only the latest and most repulsive example of that. But that has basically been the strategy since Nixon in 1968, and everybody else in the party has followed it since then.

Democrats, too, have been guilty of self-destructive behavior by hiding in a cloak of silence. They seem to fear criticizing these circumstances that cannot stand when one looks at them. Neither Democrats nor Republicans have done justice to the issue of race in our society.

GS: Would it be fair to say that in a more general social sense, we're not telling the truth to each other?

Bradley: Certainly. I think we're not telling the truth to each other because, first, there are raw stereotypes that are offensive to everybody. But then there are the comfortable stereotypes that exist under a cloak of silence that we don't really touch on because there might be disagreement. And if there's disagreement, you might be viewed as a racist, or you might be viewed as somebody who has an unnecessarily negative view.

I think you have to engage, because only through dialogue, as you said, can you get to the next level, which is understanding. Only then are you going to recognize that all of us bear some responsibility for dealing with the issue of race.

That begins with a simple question: When was the last time you had a conversation with somebody of a different race about the issue of race? If the answer is never, then you're really part of the problem. Everybody has to assume responsibility.

The gang member with his finger on the trigger has to be held accountable for his actions.

The teenage mother who has a couple of kids, and then has

another kid, has to understand that the life chances for herself and her child are greatly diminished.

The corporations have to hire and promote diverse talent and understand that it's ultimately in their own self-interest to do so. And the corporations themselves have to use their own moral power within the community to influence the other institutions of public life.

For example, let me tell you the story of an African American friend of mine. When he was a second year law student at Harvard Law School, he interned for the summer at a firm in Los Angeles, and every week a different partner in the firm would invite the group of interns over to his or her house for brunch. On this particular Sunday afternoon, my friend was driving to the partner's house, and another student, a white woman, rode in the car with him.

On his way to the partner's house, he sees flashing lights and is pulled over. One police car pulls in front of him, one police car pulls beside him, and another police car pulls behind him. They pull him out of the car, throw him down on the ground, put his arms behind him and handcuff him, and have their guns drawn on him. They then run around to the other side of the car, open the door and say to the white woman, "You're being held against your will, aren't you?"

She went hysterical. Absolutely hysterical. It took twenty minutes of pleading for them to realize that she wasn't being held against her will. The police just put their helmets back on, put on their sunglasses, and drove away.

That story is not just to illustrate the horrific behavior of the police in that situation, but to raise the question: What did the managing partner of that firm do on Monday? Did he call the police department and demand accountability? No, he didn't. Well, we all have to assume some responsibility on these matters.

The media have to have responsibility. Instead of just repeating endless stories of violence, I'd like to see some stories told of families who are teaching discipline and hard work, while raising their kids in the middle of a war zone. Ultimately, it's everyone's responsibility.

GS: The issue is complicated further when we add in the fact that this is no longer solely a black-white issue. It's becoming a spectrum, if you will—a multicolor and multicultural issue. There are projections I've read that predict that by 2050 what we call minorities will essentially be majorities, at least numerically, in our country.

Bradley: I think you're onto something that's very important. It's a fact that has yet to register with people—certainly with the white population of America. The fact is, by the year 2000, only 57 percent of the people who enter the work force are going to be native-born whites, and that means that the economic well-being of the children of white Americans is going to be determined by the talents of nonwhite Americans. That's the reality that's out there. The opportunity is that we in America have a more pluralistic society every year.

The number of Asian Americans who came to the United States doubled in the 1980s. The number of Latino Americans went up 50 percent in the 1980s. The result of all these influxes is that we have a much more diverse society. We are, in fact, the first world society. Now that's a tremendous opportunity. It's cultural enrichment. Come to my state of New Jersey where the kids who go to high school come from families that speak 120 different languages. In San Jose, California, the Vietnamese surname Nguyen is double the number of Joneses in the phone book. In Houston, Texas, there's a Korean restaurateur who serves Chinese food to a predominantly black clientele, while employing mostly Latino labor.

GS: These are "only in America."

Bradley: What we fail to see is that this is an economic opportunity, too. If we're going to have a world economy, then increasingly the management of successful international companies is going to have to be pluralistic. It's not only going to be the highest-quality, lowest-priced good, it's also going to be the good that is marketed in ways that are sensitive to the cultural rhythms of society.

Take a homogenous society, like Japan. What's their talent pool for running their economy in the long term and running their relations to the world? Well, the talent pool is the few Japanese universities. It's a narrow pool.

So what's the talent pool of a company that is going to embrace pluralism? The answer is the world. It's a much bigger talent pool. If you've got an Indonesian who can really make the grade, you can really utilize that to reach more markets in the world. And in America, we have the advantage of already having all those cultural rhythms in our country, so we don't have to have recruiting efforts all over the world to get the diversity that will allow us to compete.

GS: I'd like to turn the balance of our conversation over to remedies and solutions—the positive aspects, because there are so many positive aspects of this country. I've always felt that one of the special things, and most hopeful weapons in our arsenal, is the fact that we have a covenant that dates back to our founding documents to reach the best of our ideals.

Bradley: I would agree with that. The best way to illustrate how that has evolved is just to look at who has been able to participate in the democratic process—the vote. The Declaration of Independence implies everybody, of course, but when the Constitution was written, the only people who were allowed to vote were white males with property.

It wasn't until the 1830s and 1840s that white males without property were allowed the right to vote. And it wasn't until the 1860s that black males were allowed the right to vote. It wasn't until 1919 that women in America were allowed the right to vote. It wasn't until the 1950s and early 1960s that young people, 18–21, were allowed the right to vote. And it wasn't until the 1960s that some of the obstacles that kept people of color from participating were removed.

So if you look at our history, you see it is a pageant of democratic participation that proceeds from the assumptions embedded in the Declaration. And it takes place in a society where the institutions are flexible enough for each generation to remake the country.

GS: Let me finally ask you what you think this nation could become if we do the right things with regard to race in America.

Bradley: I think we could become the only society that can truly lead a diverse world by the example of what we've done domestically. We could realize a potential for leadership that Thomas Jefferson talked about endlessly, yet was never able to fully realize.

We can give a sense of feeling at home to anybody in the world when they arrive in America.

And we can, I think, have a power to our leadership that military hardware or secret diplomatic deals could never give. It's the triumph of the open heart and the open mind and the open society. And that ultimately is what awaits us if we can negotiate the ethnic and racial waters of our future with a skillful leader at the helm and an increasingly sensitive population with thousands of leaders of awareness in communities all across this country. No other country has this opportunity that we do. We must strive to achieve the potential of our ideals.

Originally broadcast February 8, 1993.

12

Kathleen Dalton

Getting to the Heart of Theodore Roosevelt

Teddy Roosevelt is not exactly overlooked in history, but what Kathleen Dalton does so well is to explore his core as a person: What were his real motivations? What was his real contribution? I think that she saw a much more complex human being than most people do. Dalton is the author of Theodore Roosevelt: A Strenuous Life *and of several articles on Roosevelt.*[1] *She is an associate fellow at the Charles Warren Center for Studies in American History at Harvard and a research fellow at the Gilder Lehrman Institute of American History.*

George Seay: Teddy Roosevelt emerges from your book as a man of great complexity. So this first question may seem a bit odd, but I wondered, if Teddy had written this book about himself, what would he have wanted to underline and what would he have wanted to leave out?

Dalton: I think he would agree with me that he invented the modern presidency and that he changed a lot of important things.

1. Kathleen Dalton, *Theodore Roosevelt: A Strenuous Life* (Knopf, 2002).

He would like that. He would like that I give him credit for supporting the Pure Food and Drug Act and the Meat Inspection Act, as well as trustbusting and standing up to big business and all those things. And I think he would agree with my story of how hard he fought later in life for social justice and old-age pensions and health insurance—ideas that became part of Social Security later on.

He might take some issue with my interpretation of his foreign policy. I'm a little bit more critical of imperialism and the racial undertones of the Spanish-American War, and some of his demeaning statements about people of color. I'm very different from Edmund Morris in that way. Edmund Morris writes within the empire nostalgia viewpoint, and I'm much more sympathetic with Mark Twain's view of TR's imperialism, which is that it was excessive and it was not necessarily the way we should have gone.

GS: Along those lines, this seemingly robust, adventurous, physical dynamo was actually quite ill for much of his life. The asthma wasn't just a childhood thing; it persisted throughout his life. He'd just as soon you not have discussed that, right?

Dalton: He wouldn't like people to know that. He tried to hide it. And we have evidence of a very serious illness, but he wanted to repress it and keep it quiet because his father taught him that illness was a sin. So he thought it was not manly to be vulnerable.

TR did put on a really important front for the world and I think to the degree that I get behind that exterior, he might be made uncomfortable by the book. But I think, in one sense, the thing I'm proudest about the book is that I did get so close to who he was and listened to his wife and his daughter in trying to get to the interior of TR.

GS: Roosevelt was born on the 27th of October, 1858, into New York's Knickerbocker elite. It's a family of wealth, position, and privilege, and his father becomes a kind of iconic presence, both when he was alive and after he was dead. This whole business of manliness and muscular Christianity and that kind of assertiveness—comment on that, because it seems to me these are major themes that run throughout the course of this man's life.

Dalton: It was an energizing ideology for him. It was a set of beliefs that helped him define who he was, and it was something that was not unique to TR. Basically, the muscular Christianity comes from a set of beliefs that Christianity needed to be revived and given more flesh and blood in the nineteenth century, because it was too ethereal and feminized. It's a movement that started in England but spread to America, and TR was raised with muscular Christianity as one of the core beliefs of his childhood.

To a degree, it's actually a belief system that brought athleticism to America. The United States didn't have required sports before the late-nineteenth century. And think about how important sports are to us now—organized football and baseball and so on. These are not only big businesses—they're really almost sacred recreations for us. So, muscular Christians changed America in really profound ways, and yet we never talk about what they did to America and for America.

GS: The book depicts well many of the big ideas that were animating this country and Western Europe, particularly Britain, I suppose: muscular Christianity, the whole notion of imperialism, and racialism as a way of looking at people of different color and people beyond our borders. It's not terribly surprising that he inherited this mindset, is it?

Dalton: Well, he did inherit it. Now, not everybody was as intense about it as he was. He was really a promoter of some of the ideas and getting people to worry about over-civilization. He thought we were becoming too effete.

But also part of my story is that he was very much steeped in the kind of cultural evolutionary racial ideas that the white race is superior and everybody else is down lower on the evolutionary scale. Those were the ideas pervading his time—the kind of racial superiority that informs imperialism. But TR did move away from it.

GS: There are contradictions in him that are really quite extraordinary. For example, despite believing in all this racialism, he's also a Lamarckian by virtue of being a scientist, so he has to believe that people can become other than what they have been born.

Dalton: That's right. And the fact that TR was a scientist makes him a little bit different from any other president and from many of the intellectuals of his time, because he believed that by research and theory and advancing knowledge that our knowledge would change. And so as a Lamarckian, even though people today laugh at Lamarckians, in fact he believed that you could change the potential of any group of people by environment.

So, he believed that any group could rise to equal potential. That made him more willing to say that maybe this cultural evolutionary status isn't permanent. It's a temporary one, and we're going to see people changing and growing. Especially when he looked at immigrants. He saw immigrants with good nutrition and education moving into the American mainstream, and he defended them as equal to anybody. With black-white issues, it's a little more complicated.

GS: It occurred to me that Teddy Roosevelt may be America's most fascinating president.

Dalton: Absolutely, I think. He's an intellectual, he's a soldier, he loves writers and artists. He wants a revival of American arts. He's not an easterner only—he's at home with cowboys and loves westerners. He tries to court the South, where his mother is from.

So, he's a multidimensional president, and he's an incredible character. And just hilariously funny. You hear him telling jokes and doing Irish brogue. People loved him. He was much more than your back-slapping politician because he was both a political thinker and an advocate. He covered a lot of bases.

GS: One of the interesting facts of Teddy Roosevelt's appeal is his afterlife. He's the one president whose caricatures, or at least a lot of them, are benign and project this image of buoyancy and ebullience. People see TR, and that's what they think about.

Dalton: That's right. And I think of him in character, as in *Arsenic and Old Lace,* going up and charging San Juan Hill.

GS: Bully.

Dalton: Bully. And so that makes him seem a little bit less serious and substantial. One of the challenges I've had with one group of historians is that they were trained on the approved version of TR, which is the raging adolescent, muscular Polonius—the really kind of crazy TR. And my version of TR is that he's a very substantial person.

Yes, he has an ebullient side; he's effusive, expressive, and fun. But he's quite a bright man. He's got a lot of integrity and a kind of moral purpose, even though sometimes he's really quite wrong on some issues. He's a serious moral voice in American history and people need to take him very seriously. Stop with the icon, and listen to this man and what he said.

GS: I know you took some exception to Richard Hofstadter's depiction of him.[2]

Dalton: It's Hofstadter who calls him a muscular Polonius who is the master therapist of the middle classes. To characterize him as a muscular Polonius means that he's giving this muscular-Christianity advice in a kind of nauseating way. And it's also trivializing how TR did speak to the middle classes. It's good for politicians to speak to the people. It's good for them. In a democracy, you want politicians who will have a dialogue with the people.

GS: Absolutely. And he actually mastered that business of speaking to the public because as president he had to circumvent Congress on a number of occasions, didn't he, by mobilizing public opinion, or appealing to it?

Dalton: That's right. He wouldn't have been able to create a Bureau of Corporations and Labor, the antitrust division of the Justice Department, or the Pure Food and Drug Act, if he hadn't gone over the heads of Congress and talked to the people.

And he learned to use the press office. He created the press office. He created the modern presidency that had a much larger sense of responsibility to the whole people, and not just a limited constitutional sense of "I send bills to Congress and then sign them."

He had a very broad sense of leadership—not only of public opinion, but of moral issues. Where should this country be going? What should we be worried about?

GS: It still is very difficult for me to decide where to place him on the conservative to liberal spectrum, if you will. The race

---

2. Richard Hofstadter, *The American Political Tradition and the Men Who Made It* (Knopf, 1962).

question really brings it to a point, for me. For example, he was clearly schooled in the racialism of his time. No one of his class, so to speak, could really avoid that. And yet, he also held his famous White House dinner for Booker T. Washington.

Dalton: I don't think TR was personally prejudiced, especially toward people like William Henry Lewis, who was a black lawyer, a football player, and somebody he shared ideas and politics with. Some of the black people he knew he treated as equals, and he could talk with them if he had something in common with them.

Phyllis Wheatley's work was in his book collection, and he read and knew quite a lot about African American cultural contributions and the importance of black culture in America. This, in a time when people said there was no black culture, and that blacks were inferior and not very smart. TR knew that was wrong.

GS: I began to see his life as kind of a progression leftward, if you will.

Dalton: Sometimes I describe my book as a Horatio Alger story. It's not rags-to-riches, but rather a transition from being a mainstream Victorian elite figure who just accepted all the myths and beliefs of his time to somebody who really questioned. He was moving on the same path as W.E.B. DuBois who said, "Give us a chance. Everybody has equal potential." And TR was moving, based on his experience and his reading, toward seeing, by the end of his life, equal potential and humanity in people of all ethnic groups, even those that were downtrodden. And he wanted the government to be an active force for good. He wanted government to be for social justice.

GS: I'm reminded that he was perhaps our most intensely moralistic president.

Dalton: Absolutely. In some sense, I think that's why he cared so much about social justice. I think progressives were generally pulled into reform in part because of moral concerns and in part because of a religious atmosphere. And that's part of the mood of the age. He argued that you had to pay a living wage to women workers because that's the only thing that would stop them from going into prostitution. So, he got to the living wage in advocacy of women workers from a moral route.

He got into old-age insurance and unemployment insurance because he said people would turn to gambling, drinking, and prostitution if they didn't have things that would pull them into middle-class life. That's a classically progressive outlook, and it's one of the reasons we got so many reform ideas out of that generation.

GS: Internationally, he produced what I call remarkable and contrasting results. He was aggressive in securing the Panama Canal, diplomatic in the Portsmouth Treaty ending the Russo-Japanese War (for which he won the Nobel Peace Prize, the first American to do so), forceful in his corollary to the Monroe Doctrine, yet paternalistic and somewhat interventionist in terms of Latin America. What's your verdict?

Dalton: My verdict is that all of that is true. There certainly were two sides of TR's foreign policy. One is imperialistic and kind of condescending to Latin America—intervening in the Caribbean a lot, and with Panama, not a moment of respect for Latin American sovereignty. But on the other hand, he was an advocate of international organizations before Woodrow Wilson, and he argued for a League of Nations and tried to get Latin America included in international tribunals and the Central American Court of Justice.

Later in life, he saw that we needed international structures of government and law to help organize conflict resolution and also to prevent war. And he was a really effective diplomatic peacemaker. So, he's very complicated in terms of foreign policy, such that people who stereotype him as just a warmonger miss the point.

GS: Lastly, what's on my mind is that this is a presidential election year, and people all over the place are invoking the name Teddy Roosevelt. Local politicians will do it and national politicians do it. What contributions and qualities of his are most important for remembrance and emulation in this political year for our country?

Dalton: I think TR was a true democrat—a small "d" democrat—in some of the same ways that Thomas Jefferson was. He really believed in government by the people and that people should rule. And I think he was very worried about special privilege and he hated the media moguls who told people what to think.

I guess if TR were to speak from the grave to us, he would be outraged by the fact that America now has only four or five media conglomerates telling us what to think about every moment. The primary system has really been corrupted by the media and I think we're not getting to choose. Pundits are telling us what to think.

Teddy Roosevelt was an emotional man because he would get angry about injustices, and I think in an election year where one candidate in particular [Howard Dean] has been eliminated because of showing his emotion in the wrong way, I think that TR wouldn't like that one bit. Anger and emotion are really how we handle things we feel very strongly about, and we should feel very strongly about American politics. It's our life and our children's lives. So, I think TR would argue for more democracy and fewer pundits.

Originally broadcast March 29, 2004.

13

Kristie Miller

Isabella Greenway's Politics
on the Frontier

In 1992, Kristie Miller published a biography on her grandmother, Ruth Hanna McCormick, who served as an Illinois congresswoman in the late 1920s. Since then, she has dedicated herself to showcasing the lives and accomplishments of America's pioneering political women. Her most recent biography, Isabella Greenway: An Enterprising Woman, *was named the 2004 Southwest Book of the Year and won the Willa Award for Nonfiction in 2005.[1]*

�֍

George Seay: Kristie, let me start off with an overall perception of this book and this life we're about to discuss. Isabella Greenway's life combines hardship and privilege, both of which she seems to have met graciously throughout her time. Her parents, Tilden and Patty Selmes, moved from Minnesota to the Dakota Territory in the last quarter of the nineteenth century. Can you comment on my perception of her dealing with both hardship and privilege, as well as the importance of the frontier? I get the feeling that she never really left it.

---

1. Kristie Miller, *Isabella Greenway: An Enterprising Woman* (University of Arizona Press, 2004).

Miller: She did not spend that much time on the frontier because her parents, who became close friends of Theodore Roosevelt when they were all ranchers in the Dakota Territory, were, also like Teddy, economically wiped out by the blizzard of 1886. This was right after Isabella was born. She actually spent less than a year in the Dakota Territory with her parents.

Her great aunt, Julia Dinsmore, who had raised her mother, lived on a farm just outside Cincinnati in Boone County, Kentucky. That was still a pretty rough place to grow up. They grew tobacco. It was kind of marginal farming, and so she was no stranger to hardship. Her father died when she was nine, after which her mother really did not have any money at all and never had a home of her own. But she didn't really grow up on the sort of frontier as those early Dakota beginnings might suggest. But I think that the feeling of the plains did remain with her all her life.

GS: I was speaking more metaphorically, I suppose. I get this "I will confront life and life will not beat me down" spirit from her, which we associate, I think rightly, with the frontier spirit. It seems to be a part of her from day one to the end, even though she didn't physically reside there for a great length of time. The other part of my notion, which does have a kind of physical embodiment, is the fact that the West seems to be powerfully important to her as not just a place, but a theme and a canvas for her interests throughout her life.

Miller: Certainly. She had to move out further west to Silver City, New Mexico, in 1910 when her first husband, Robert Ferguson, was diagnosed with tuberculosis, and they were really roughing it then. They lived in tents for several years because there was lots of fresh air, and that was considered to be an important part of the cure for tuberculosis at the time.

Eventually, they built a beautiful house there—Isabella had fantastic architectural tendencies. But she, especially because she was the much younger wife of a desperately ill man, really ran the ranch there, took care of and home-schooled the children, and really did everything. And I think that kind of independence and necessity did give her an unusual pioneer spirit that translated into everything she did, including being a pioneer politician.

GS: She had this tremendous spirit of independence and ability to cope with hardship. Yet, though her background, at least monetarily, didn't seem to be terribly privileged, she was, through her background and her family, very well connected.

Miller: I think she was very well connected in two respects. One was the friendship with the Roosevelts. Roosevelt's biographer David McCullough once said that if Roosevelt and Isabella's mother, Patty Selmes, had ever been single at the same time, something certainly would have come of it. There was this strong mutual attraction. But Roosevelt was a widower when he met Patty and Tilden Selmes. When Tilden Selmes died, Roosevelt had remarried.

Patty Selmes ended up moving to New York in order to live with her sister and her brother-in-law, who was a successful attorney. He was the one who made it possible for Isabella to go to a good girls' finishing school and to make a debut.

But it was a very Edith Wharton sort of story, because there were undertones of tragedy throughout her life, and that debut was almost a financial necessity. The idea of investing in her dresses was so she could marry a wealthy, or at least successful, husband.

GS: What I also find interesting is that, at the time of that debut, or shortly thereafter, when she is in the New York whirl, she's already telling her friends and peers that social issues are important.

Miller: After her father died when she was nine, it left her with a feeling of great responsibility for her mother, and she was often very introspective, especially when she visited her father's grave site in Kentucky. She would reflect that we were put here on earth to take care of people.

She and Eleanor Roosevelt, who became her friend when they were both in their teens, and Mary Harriman were founders of the Junior League, which at the time was a social welfare organization. I think it still is, although it now has some connotations of being more of a society enterprise. But this was a very serious endeavor at the turn of the century, in which Isabella participated.

GS: She also had a beautiful command of the English language, didn't she, Kristie? She was eloquent with her expressions and, sometimes, when she wanted to bring someone down to size, she could speak in a very cutting manner. I'm not certain I've read all that much about her formal education. What was her educational background?

Miller: She went to a girls' school and did not actually graduate because she said she kept waiting for the head mistress to realize that Latin was not useful to a young girl, and it just never happened. So, she was self-educated, insofar as she was.

But I think that many politicians, especially of that era, were people who learned directly from people rather than from books. She had a few books that she admired very much. She thought Emerson was the greatest writer of all time, and she read his essays over and over. But I don't see much about her reading or educating herself in that manner.

She listened to people and talked to people, and had a very democratic choice of friends. She was friends with everybody —from farmers in the tobacco country, to ranch hands in the West, and the swells in New York society. She could feel comfortable with them all.

GS: I was struck by the number of people who were mentioned or quoted in the latter chapters, some of whom were merely children of people who knew her. Many of these were children of people who knew her when their circumstances were humble and they were miners or ranchers. They thought the world of her.

Miller: Yes. It's absolutely essential, it seems to me, for anyone who does succeed in politics to be able to make a person feel that he or she is the most important person in the world when that politician is talking to him or her, and Isabella had this ability of being able to focus intensely on a single person and see his potential.

GS: I want now to quote briefly from the book something which I think might give even further insight into what was so remarkable about this woman. It's from an early chapter in the book, where Isabella makes the surprising discovery that she "had the makings of a man within and the glory of a woman concealing it. One must have some men's common sense to know when to be the woman. It takes some time to judge. I've made up my mind to be a man for at least five years, probably longer."

That's so interesting. It's not the way a woman would phrase this in our time, but I think the meaning is very clear. She saw herself as no less than anyone else on this earth and certainly as capable of bringing forth all the strength to meet any challenge life would give her, no matter what society was going to tell her to do.

Miller: Yes, that was at the time when she was in New Mexico, taking care of her ill husband and having to do a lot of things and make a lot of decisions that were not particularly common for a woman at that time. I think it's very emblematic that she headed up something called the Women's Land Army in New Mexico around that time. These were women who went out to harvest crops when the men were away fighting in World War I.

They called it potato patriotism. And it was not without risk, because the 1918 influenza epidemic was raging around the countryside and a lot of the people she was working with got sick, and some died, and she, feeling feverish on occasion and thinking she might be catching influenza, would dose herself with quinine.

But I think this high identification with the things that men did was again, as you observed, something that carried over later in her life and helped her to step in and take over men's roles, whether it be in the fields or in Congress.

GS: World War I played an important role in her life. She really came to identify with veterans' issues, and she turned those feelings into actions in a very entrepreneurial way.

Miller: Yes. Her second husband, John Greenway, was a real hero in World War I, as he had been in the Spanish-American War. He received a brevet promotion to general at the end of the war, and after his death she wanted to have contact with the veterans who came to Arizona in great numbers. Many of them came because there was still no cure for tuberculosis, and she used to go to the hospitals to visit them.

One time she went and discovered that they were making little knickknacks to sell in order to generate some kind of income. This was before all of the social welfare programs of the New Deal. She was a person who was very interested in art and architecture, so she promised them she would buy their output for three months. Well, the next morning she woke up and read in the newspaper that she had started a new business. So, she decided that she needed a factory, persuaded the mayor to give her an empty church, and installed the veterans and members of their families there and created a furniture factory.

GS: Isabella called it "The Hut," correct?

Miller: The Hut was a slang term for the place where the dough boys in World War I went for rest and relaxation, so she thought that would be an attractive name. Unfortunately, with the onset of the Depression, the business failed. She had to keep buying up the furniture. Finally somebody said to her, "What are you going to do with all that furniture—open a hotel?"
    And she said, "Good idea!"

GS: I'm laughing, but in point of fact this is another major chapter and accomplishment in her life. She built the Arizona Inn, which survives to this day as one of the leading establishments in this country.

Miller: Absolutely. It's on the Zagat's best hundred hotels list. It's going to be seventy-five years old next year and is run by her granddaughter, who adheres to all of Isabella's notions of privacy, comfort, and service. It's an absolutely idyllic place. She managed to update it without losing any of the old charm that was characteristic of the inn in Isabella's day.

GS: You know, even if Isabella had only established the Arizona Inn, and even if she had only—and this is another thing she did entrepreneurially—owned and operated an airline, it would be worth writing a book about her. But this is only part of what she did.

I want to focus on The Hut a bit longer, in this sense. In addition to being what it was physically, I also took it to be the embodiment of her notion of putting her politics into action. Talk about her sense of politics that would lead her to go from Teddy Roosevelt's politics to FDR's politics, an evolution which is quite dramatic.

Miller: I think that as Teddy Roosevelt got older, he became more progressive, and by the end of his life he was, in many ways, quite radical in his thinking. Isabella got her start in politics by campaigning for Teddy Roosevelt in the 1912 election, when he was running on the Progressive or Bull Moose ticket, and she didn't even have the right to vote yet. New Mexico had just become a state, and they had not given women the franchise, but she went around and registered voters and talked up Roosevelt to his former Rough Riders in New Mexico, and found that it was a really exciting thing to do.

I think you're right that the impulse that led her to open The Hut is that you should take care of people and see that there was equity and that they got a fair shake. And that was the hallmark of the New Deal legislation. She and Eleanor frequently beat up on FDR, to try to push him to be more progressive and more liberal than he knew he was going to be able to be, given the political realities. So, I think of the FDR policies in a way being an evolution of the later Theodore Roosevelt policies.

GS: And in that context, she represents continuity between the two.

Miller: She does, because she had known Theodore Roosevelt in the Bad Lands. She was a bridesmaid in Franklin and Eleanor's wedding, and a close friend of theirs for their whole lives after that. Eleanor really recruited Isabella into the Democratic Party; she had been a Bull Moose Republican until 1920. In 1924, she became so appalled by the conservatism of the Republicans that she became a Democrat, and Eleanor recruited her to help elect FDR.

GS: Which she does. In 1932, she speaks at the Democratic Convention very powerfully and eloquently on his behalf, and in a kind of a nitty-gritty combat sense, she gets the California delegation to support him, which was absolutely essential to his becoming the nominee and then the president.

Miller: That was the most exciting part of the research for this book, George, because I knew about the Inn, I knew that she'd been in Congress, I knew about the airline company, but I hadn't realized that she had a real role in the "California Switch," as it was called, and I was not just fancying this.

The *Time* magazine article that ran when she was elected herself, in 1933, as Arizona's only congressperson, referred to her as having a hand in that switch. The man that she lobbied was also given credit by FDR's campaign manager, Jim Farley, as being one of the two people most responsible for that switch, which really did guarantee FDR's nomination. Today, looking with hindsight at four consecutive elections, his presidency may have seemed like an inevitability, but it by no means was.

GS: I'm certain that fueled her own political fires. What kind of congresswoman was Isabella?

Miller: She worked very hard for her constituents. I'd say that was what most of her activities were taken up with. She worked very hard to make sure the veterans did not lose their benefits during the initial cost-cutting phase of the New Deal, when they were trying to balance the budget across the board. She argued that that absolutely could not be done in the case of tubercular veterans. She helped people get mortgages for their homes and farms. She brought a lot of work to Arizona. Arizona had more Civilian Conservation Corps camps than any other state per capita.

They also got a lot of money for WPA [Works Progress Administration] projects. She got money to finish Route 66, and she worked very hard on some of the difficult issues concerning grazing rights, water rights, and the Indian reservations. That was a time of great flux in America's policy toward Native Americans, and she was on the House Committee for Indian Affairs and very active in that.

GS: At one point she actually breaks with FDR, doesn't she, without breaking the friendship with him, right? How does she do that?

Miller: She was elected in part because she would have access to the president. It was seen as an advantage for the state of Arizona that she was going to be able to just hit the ground running and have this close relationship with the executive. Newspapers said she would have a latchkey to the White House, and in fact, she went over there all the time because she was such a close friend of both of theirs—particularly of Eleanor's.

But she wanted to be sure that that friendship was never a liability for her, and that she would not be held responsible for any of the administration's mistakes. I think that was her political judgment. But I think, at the same time, she had this real fervor for progressive ideas.

FDR was a consummate politician, and he would usually try for whatever he thought he could get, and he would not break his heart trying for things that he knew were never going to pass the Senate. So, sometimes she would break with him on the issues that he was not supporting that she thought he should support. Eventually, this culminated in her not supporting him in the 1940 election. She felt that a third term was something that shouldn't happen—that this broke with precedent too much— so she supported Wendell Willkie. I've heard conflicting stories about whether she really was able to maintain a friendship with

FDR after that, though she certainly did with Eleanor, because to Eleanor, politics never really got in the way of friendship.

GS: I always end a conversation about a biography by asking the obvious question about a legacy and the meaning of the person's life and what one should take away from it.

Miller: I think in the East—and I'm basically from the East—there's a tendency to overlook western women, which I think is regrettable on two counts. For one, you don't want to overlook anybody who contributes to this country. But also, the West was actually a much friendlier place for women in politics than the East. I think the kind of people who went west were people who were mold-breakers to begin with, and frequently the rigors of the West killed off the men, which forced the women to cope, just as Isabella did.

Isabella was only the seventeenth woman in Congress—that was still a very small group of people. One of her political advisers in New York said, "You were fortunate to be from the West because you can achieve things that somebody here in New York would have a much harder time achieving."

And I think that's true, that these western women really set a standard for the rest of the United States to follow. They really were pioneers in more than the physical sense of breaking new ground. Recall that suffrage came first in the West.

Another thing that really struck me is after I had basically done the research for this book, I read Sandra Day O'Connor's memoir, and in that memoir, she writes that she grew up on a ranch that straddled the New Mexico–Arizona border, very close to Silver City where Isabella homesteaded.[2] O'Connor said that when she was a child her family used to go to this old homestead in

2. Sandra Day O'Connor and H. Alan Day, *Lazy B: Growing Up on a Cattle Ranch in the American Southwest* (Random House, 2002).

New Mexico to cut their Christmas tree, and that it was a place where Theodore Roosevelt had visited. Now that has to be Isabella's homestead. So there's this connection, and of course O'Connor became an attorney in Phoenix and learned all about Isabella, so I think Isabella's greatest legacy is that she was a role model for Sandra Day O'Connor. The governor of Arizona today is Janet Napolitano. There are all these wonderful western women in politics today who have Isabella to thank in some way.

Originally broadcast February 14, 2005.

14

Godfrey Hodgson
American Conservatism
and Its Many Faces

Godfrey Hodgson is a British journalist who loves America.
But I've always had the feeling that he thought Americans
don't examine their own experiences enough even when, because
of our power, everything we do enormously affects other people.
Hodgson has worked as a newspaper and magazine journalist,
a television reporter, a documentary maker, a news anchor,
and a university teacher. He has written a number of books,
including a major biography of Senator Daniel Patrick Moynihan.
His book on the conservative movement, The World Turned
Right Side Up, *came out in 1996.*[1]

❈

George Seay: It's a terrific pleasure to have the chance to talk
with you about a book that I think is a very important one for
all of us. You argue that there was a process of redefinition that
took place just after World War II, in which conservatives
began to define first, liberalism, and then, conservatism. Is that
correct?

---

1. Godfrey Hodgson, *The World Turned Right Side Up: A History of the Conservative Ascendancy in America* (Houghton Mifflin, 1996).

Hodgson: I think that's right. I'm reminded of the phrase of Disraeli's, which, among others, Irving Kristol and Daniel Patrick Moynihan are very fond of, that goes, "With words we govern men." And I think there has been a tendency in the United States to underestimate the power of ideas and the power of words, which is the only clothing in which ideas can walk around.

GS: You certainly point out that importance in your book. Another theme that runs through it is that the streams of conservatism, perhaps joined by their mutual rejection of liberalism, had to come together and flow over the course of these past several decades to make everything happen.

Hodgson: Well, I was trying to describe that convergence, or that confluence. I use the metaphor—probably overuse the metaphor, actually—of the river, but I was also suggesting that there are contradictory strands in American conservatism; that there is, for example, an obvious conflict between the traditionalist, rather authoritarian, religious and moral conservative tradition and the libertarian tradition, in particular its corporate economic version.

In other words, it really won't do, I went on to argue, to blame liberals for loose sexual mores, for hedonism, and for the breakup of the family, when corporate pressures—advertising, marketing, and the like—have had at least as much, in my opinion, to do with those problems. So I was, from the beginning, suggesting not only that conservatism was coming from different sources, but that it would eventually be heading in different directions.

GS: An early chapter in your book is entitled "Headwaters," and that of course conveys this metaphor of the convergence of the streams that we're going to be following here. It deals with the conservative intellectuals and authors who were writing in and around the 1940s, people like Ayn Rand, Albert J. Nock, Friedrich Hayek, and Russell Kirk. These were very different people, writing very different books, but they all laid the foundation intellectually for what would become a conservative convergence and ascendancy. Now it's a big question as to how they differ, but what is the common message among them? What's the underlying union?

Hodgson: I could, of course, have taken other writers of that decade who have proven to be influential in the origins of the conservative intellectual movement. One thinks of Leo Strauss, who's enjoying a kind of cult status, almost, at the moment, and certainly he was an influential writer. And there are others. Karl Popper, for example. I focus on those four because they seem to me to demonstrate the really profound contradictions between these different conservative traditions.

Ayn Rand, for example, was a writer who believed in the dynamism of capitalism. She almost ferociously worshiped competitive individualism. She admired the world of skyscrapers and machinery and manufacturing and she liked material well being —even material excess.

Albert J. Nock, on the other hand, absolutely despised that world. In his most famous book, *The Memoirs of a Superfluous Man* (University Press of America, 2002), he actually compares by name Henry Ford and Thomas Alva Edison to animals, and suggests that the economic man in the United States has abandoned civilization.

GS: These intellectual figures, and then as the progression continued, these politicians, religious figures, and others, paraded before my view almost like actors on a stage. My metaphor, of course, begs the question of what the backdrop was. I thought it fundamentally important that as the late forties turned into the fifties, the background was the Cold War and the McCarthy period.

Hodgson: Absolutely right. I think the background is a contrast between a 1950s America which is bursting with economic juices and is conscious of its power, and at the same time, suffering from this almost paranoid feeling.

Why is that? We've won World War II, we've become the most powerful country in the world, and yet, somehow, we're actually feeling more vulnerable than we ever were before. There was a feeling that somebody must have betrayed us.

Now of course, it actually is true. It has become increasingly plain from the Venona tapes and other new evidences that have come up that there was treason. It probably wasn't overwhelmingly important, and it would have been better if people had stayed calm about it, but the liberal take on what happened simply isn't sustainable anymore.

In any case, the 1950s were a period of enormous prosperity and the realization of at least the first dreams of enormous numbers of ordinary people, combined with an atmosphere of sour suspicion, resentment, and conformity—this deep desire not to step out of line in any way for fear of being thought to be tainted with communism, foreign or domestic.

I think that it's quite an important thing, actually. The intellectuals were afraid of foreign communism—real communism, if you wish—the Soviet Union and its captive nations. And the business conservatives were afraid of domestic communism, by which they meant unionism, aggressive behavior on the part of the unions, and of the liberals.

The events of the 1960s and 1970s in the United States were a powerful traumatic shock for a great many Americans, and not least for a great many liberal intellectuals. They saw the civil rights movement, which they thought they had been in favor of, turning into demands for economic equality, a goal that was much harder to accept.

They saw the campaign to contain, and eventually roll back, communism turning into what was pretty hard to distinguish from an aggressive colonial war.

They saw the domestic tranquility shaken by the assassination of a president, the assassination of Martin Luther King, and the assassination of the president's brother, but they also saw street rioting and, generally, a wilder, harsher, less tranquil society. This was as traumatic as it was because of the high claims which they had made and the high hopes which they cherished of what American society was going to be. The idea was, after all, based on a rather profound idea that America was going to be the "Great Society," to borrow Lyndon Johnson's slogan.

GS: To carry the story into the 1970s, it's a mood, I thought, and I think your book makes this point, that Jimmy Carter didn't fully grasp. One example of this was the misperception he had when he talked of a malaise among the American people. The real feeling was one of deep disappointment, anger, and resentment, and a wish to reassert a better America.

Hodgson: I think that's right. There's a detail which I think is quite important. I wrote an article in which I asserted that we came very close to a major realignment in American politics, which was headed off by Watergate.

I have evidence that there were very advanced negotiations about whether or not some forty conservative southern Democrats were going to cross the floor and become Republicans. And the same thing was, after all, happening elsewhere in society, and after President Nixon's smashing victory in 1972, I think we might have seen a conservative realignment eight years earlier than it happened; or, if you like, a "Reagan revolution" under Nixon.

Now if that's right, then it means that the issues that would have brought about a conservative realignment in '72 would have been different from the issues that brought it about in the 1980s. There had been eight further years of deep unhappiness for tens of millions of Americans, symbolized, in a way, I suppose, by the gas lines of 1974, the humiliating end of the war in Vietnam in '75, and a whole series of other painful and traumatizing events.

And that meant that when President Reagan finally put it together and sort of marched the motley armies of conservatism through the gates of the captured city of Washington, they were thinking about significantly different things from what the Nixon people would have been thinking of in 1973.

GS: Let's stay with Ronald Reagan and the time just before he took office. I want to emphasize this point because I think it is crucial in the book. I counted four major things that were coming together at the time that Ronald Reagan arrived and was able to symbolize and advance them. The first was a decline of pride and place; the general sense of the loss of Vietnam, and the oil shocks.

Hodgson: The Panama Canal.

GS: The Panama Canal, certainly. And second would be the economic issues that derive from that kind of uncertainty. Third were the social issues—abortion, desegregation, the race question continually. And fourth was the driving force of religious fundamentalism. Am I right on that, or are there more?

Hodgson: Yes, and I think you can chop them up in different ways. It is passionately denied by conservatives that racial feelings, or the desires to preserve a racial status quo, had anything to do with their ideas. This may well be true of individual leaders. But it seems to me that there is no question that a fundamental part of this revolution was shifts in the South. In particular, the South ceased to be the Democratic South. However conservative they had been on social issues, they had been liberal on economic issues. But now it has increasingly become the Republican South. That is one important part of what happened.

In a sense, you could also say that what was happening was the southernization of the United States. We talk on a day when some tens, if not hundreds, of thousands of young people in New York have gone to a country and western concert with great enthusiasm. That would have been inconceivable twenty years ago. That's only a tiny symbol of the way in which southern white working class mores, which were peripheral and provincial, have actually in some ways become mainstream.

GS: New Yorkers were all saying they were from New Jersey.

Hodgson: Absolutely. And, of course, we've also now got a Congress which is overwhelmingly run by conservative white southern Republicans, as opposed to one in which the driving force came from northern white Democratic liberals who were restrained, more or less, by southern white conservative Democrats. So there has been a kind of southernization both of the culture and of the political system, which I think awaits its historian. It's a huge and fascinating story.

By the way, I love the South enough in many ways to think that hasn't been all bad. I think there are some very attractive aspects of southern culture, which includes a certain directness, a certain verbal and literary talent and felicity.

GS: I'm wondering, as you speak, though, how you characterize the importance of Ronald Reagan to all of this. That's a big question, but was that the genius of that particular moment in the conservative ascendancy: the ability to mount this superb and sublime symbol of all they stood for in the person of Ronald Reagan, a symbol for all these forces that were coalescing?

Hodgson: I believe so. I made a series of three television documentaries about President Reagan in 1988, near the end of his time, and I was immensely impressed by the skill with which he articulated this upbeat uniting vision of America.

GS: At least fundamentally, what he did first was to capture the public imagination, to symbolize that.

Hodgson: I think so. I think he also understood how people—how tens of millions, a majority—felt, because he felt that way himself. I think he was a very straightforward man in some ways. He could be extremely skillful as a communicator and so forth.

I do not, by the way, subscribe to the view that Ronald Reagan was an unintelligent man. I think in many ways he had a powerful grasp of big ideas. I think he's a very, very enigmatic and interesting political figure, but I also think he's a very important figure. I think he articulated things—simple ideas which largely proved to be true.

For example, one was that people wanted not only less taxation, but less government. Another was that the Soviet Union was a fraud; that it wasn't the great powerful juggernaut which it had been in a lot of people's interest to pretend that it was. You know, what President Eisenhower called the military-industrial complex had every interest in believing that the Soviet Union really was as big and fierce and dangerous as they said. Ronald Reagan sort of had a shrewd hunch that it might not be so.

GS: And in point of fact, he was right.

Hodgson: He was right, although again, I think it's quite important not to attribute the collapse of communism entirely to the successful policies of the Reagan administration. A certain number of very courageous people inside the communist world deserve some credit for that, too.

But Reagan is a strange man because at the middle level—you

may remember I rather rudely compared him to an inverted sandwich. At the top level, there are these two or three powerful ideas, and at the bottom level, there's a good deal of skill in terms of the presentation of a speech or his ability to know how to deal with all kinds of people, including politicians.

And in the middle, there is this kind of soggy wedge of indifference to technical matters. He actually said to me, when I interviewed him, "You know, I have lots of clever people who can do that kind of thing for me."

GS: Does all this amount to, in your opinion, a Reagan revolution?

Hodgson: That is a question I find difficult to answer. It does seem to me that the center of gravity in American politics and the politics of ideas in America has shifted a number of points to the right, and, probably, irreversibly, at least for a considerable period of time. That, I think, is different from suggesting, "Well, that's it. The game's over. We won."

One of my motives in writing this book, actually, was my considerable irritation with the kind of triumphalism of the intellectuals of the right who really wanted their own history written only by people who were converted to their point of view, who underestimated their failures and their divisions, and presented a kind of propagandistic advertising view of the thing. That always irritated me, and still does.

But, yes, there was a real shift. I think the central issue has to do with the legitimacy of government. If I am not conservative, at least not in the sense in which American conservatives now use the word, it's because I do not believe that government—that is to say, democratically elected government—is necessarily identical with something called the state. The American conservatives seem to me to caricature government as something carried out by men in long black leather overcoats with pistols in their belts.

I don't think that the government, or indeed I'll be bold and use the word state, is necessarily bad. The questions are: How effective is it? How well run is it? How well does it reflect the interests or wishes of the people? And you occasionally read in the right-wing columnists and other works that it would be wonderful if the state virtually disappeared. It's an ironic echo of the Marxists themselves, who said the state was going to wither away.

I think there are two things which I find comical about that. One is that these people affect to despise the state, but they love the FBI, and they love the Army Corps of Engineers, and they love the Air Force, but these are all parts of the state. If they limited themselves to saying we should have a serious discussion about which activities should be publicly carried out and which should be privately carried out, that would be fine. But in fact there's a kind of propaganda against the whole notion of the public role, which seems to me to have gone too far.

The other thing which kind of makes me laugh is the idea that only the state is characterized by something very bad called bureaucracy. Well, if you ever have any dealings with a bank, an insurance company, or an airline, you will find that they are at least as bureaucratic as the federal government, I dare say.

GS: As we conclude this conversation, I want to ask if the recent conflicts among conservatives suggest that these streams that you have so artfully described as flowing together may now begin to be under some danger of starting to fall apart?

Hodgson: The image would be of a great river which ends not in a single mouth, but in a delta, like the Mississippi or the Nile. I suppose I instinctively feel that no single political movement can express the variety and energies of American society; that there are just too many strands there—conservative strands and other strands; that any attempt to impose a kind of ideological orthodoxy—which, to some extent, the conservative foundations have tried to do—is just doomed to failure. The country is too complicated and too independent. Americans are just not willing to be told what they're supposed to think, or what to believe, and their interests are so divergent. So I think an attempt to maintain a conservative orthodoxy is doomed.

The interesting thing about the rebellion so far is that, on the whole, it's been the right that's been rebelling against even the slightest sign of accommodationism or moderation on the parts of the Republican leadership. And if it's to hold onto its very promising prospects of power, it will have to learn to be a little bit less ideologically purist and to accommodate different strands and, indeed, to deal with and confront nonconservative forces in American life.

But if you ask me what the most urgent and serious order of business at the moment is, my instinct would be that it's trying to create a new and realistic liberalism. I have long felt that the old New Deal, or post–New Deal liberalism, had run into the sand. There were these sort of instinctive arrangements whereby whenever anybody announced that there was a problem in society, an agency was created. You staffed the agency and threw money at the problem and the problem was supposed to disappear. And that didn't work.

So I think the great merit of a group of people called the neoconservatives—people associated with a magazine like *The Public Interest,* for example—is that they asked very tough questions and very shrewd questions about whether these liberal solutions were actually going to work. That questioning, however, has now been carried out, and it seems to me the new question is: Given that we cannot really do without government in a modern society, and given that there are some things that the private sector cannot do, or at least cannot do without guidance from democratically elected leaders, then what are the techniques? What are the solutions? How can government and private enterprises work together more effectively to deal with issues, such as unfairness and inequality and deprivation?

Originally broadcast October 20, 1997.

15

Joan Biskupic

An Insider's View of the U.S. Supreme Court

With degrees in law and journalism, Joan Biskupic has covered the Supreme Court for the Congressional Quarterly, *the* Washington Post, *and* USA Today. *She has been particularly intrigued by Sandra Day O'Connor's fiery spirit and great influence on the Court, leading to a biography of O'Connor, which traces a path to national prominence that began long before Reagan chose her.[1] Here Biskupic describes the workings of the Court and the interplay of personality and ideology.*

✺

George Seay: I want to really understand how the Supreme Court, what some call "The Marble Palace," works. It's so beautiful and so columned, and it suggests the very majesty of justice itself, which is at the heart of our democratic system, when you get down to it.

---

1. Joan Biskupic, *Sandra Day O'Connor: How the First Woman on the Supreme Court Became Its Most Influential Justice* (ECCO, 2005).

Biskupic: It certainly does. It's a place that has its own distinct customs and rituals, and I think it's worth drawing back the crimson velvet curtains every now and then to look at the individual nine justices there.

GS: That's why I'm so excited about this conversation. Before we talk about individual justices, though, let's discuss how cases get into that marble palace in the first place. What's the route by which they begin to be considered by the court?

Biskupic: That's a good question, because actually about 7,000 cases arrive on their doorstep each year, and they only take about 80 or 90 of those cases, and then issue rulings in about 75.

Cases come up through the federal system and through state courts. The main way is that if these come through a federal District Court, they start with a trial judge who listens to the case and the losing party will typically appeal to an appellate court. That's our second level. The losing party can then appeal to the Supreme Court.

Now, the Supreme Court is not obligated to take any of these appeals. What it looks for are conflicts in the different circuit courts. For example, if one of these regional circuits covering the West Coast has ruled differently from a circuit covering the East Coast. But then it also looks for questions of national importance.

The justices are often looking to settle questions of great national importance or ones where it's really important for the justices to clarify something. For example, a case involving separation of powers, or an act of Congress—especially when an act of Congress has been struck down. There's a certain urgency for the nation's highest court to at least look at it.

GS: Joan, I've heard the phrase "original jurisdiction." Quite frankly, I don't know what it means, but I've grappled with it. Does it mean that the justices can also, and in a kind of separate path, select anything just because they want to?

Biskupic: No, they can never select anything just because they want to. Something has to be a case or a controversy. Something actually has to come to them. They can't just offer advisory opinions. But they can, for example, in terms of states versus states over boundaries or water lines—things like that— those come up through a separate track. So that's what you're referring to there. But they can never just reach out.

Part of what the Constitution says, along with that magnificent language you read, is that the Supreme Court can only decide a case or controversy. It can't just jump in and say, "You know, we don't really like the way President Bush, or President Clinton, is doing something right now." It has to come through some sort of legal structure. And even if it comes to the court as a matter of original jurisdiction, it's still posed as two parties in dispute over something in law.

GS: You said there were some 7,000 cases, but only 75 or so ultimately get ruled upon by the court, which means an enormous number don't make it, obviously. Can they come back, or are they out of the game when they're not selected the first time?

Biskupic: The Supreme Court is the highest court in the land, and once you are out of the game, you've got nowhere else to go. At that point, your only recourse is to try to get something changed legislatively.

GS: You know, I'm really fascinated by this next question, Joan, and it's kind of an obvious one for a lay person who hasn't gotten past those red curtains you mentioned. What's the workday like up there? How do these sessions really operate? What goes on inside?

Biskupic: That's a great question, because people don't know. The Supreme Court is open to the public on a daily basis, but the justices hold oral arguments only during set times, and that's the only time you can see them. And you can't go back and see them in chambers, although because I cover the court, I'm lucky enough to see that.

They all come in early in the morning and they do different things. Justice O'Connor first goes to an exercise class that's up in the gym on the top floor of the Supreme Court. Other justices do different things.

Clarence Thomas, when they don't have oral arguments, will often telecommute. He's very computer-savvy, so he often telecommutes.

So they all come in, and, on days that they're hearing arguments, at ten o'clock the buzzer sounds and they all come out behind these crimson curtains and they take seats. But before they do that, they shake hands all around. And before they're in their private conferences to actually decide cases, they also shake hands all around. It's been a tradition, and some of them say it especially helps to minimize the personal disagreements among them.

And then they hear cases from the bench, and that's open to the public. And then on days of oral arguments, they'll go to the justices' dining room and have lunch together, and they talk over lunch about things that you and I talk about over lunch—movies, the weather, and the like.

GS: But not the job.

Biskupic: Right. They talk about things that won't go into the substance of the case. And then in the afternoon they all work in various manners. David Souter, for example, an appointee by the first George Bush, likes to do drafts of opinion in longhand. Some of them work on computers. Stephen Breyer is very computer-savvy. He's got the court computer set up, and then he's got a bunch of laptops set up, too. And he's always going on *Orbitz* to find some deal for travel.

There are four slots for law clerks, and each of the justices works closely with their four clerks.

GS: And these are extremely prestigious positions, aren't they?

Biskupic: Oh, very much so. The clerkships are very competitive, and typically, these individuals are the cream of the crop from our law schools and they've already had jobs clerking for Appeals Court judges. Remember, again, the hierarchy of the judicial system. The Supreme Court justices like to see individuals who have had experience writing opinions at the next step down—the federal Appeals Court levels. And so these individuals help the justices draft opinions, and they help the justices decide which cases to take.

Chief Justice William Rehnquist has many outside interests, so he tends to knock off work fairly early—before dinner time. Justice Harry Blackman, who was on the court until 1994, had a habit of working late into the night. Several of them bring work home with them.

At Justice William Brennan's funeral, his son, in his eulogy, talked about Justice Brennan setting up a card table late at night, after having dinner, and working on things.

Justice O'Connor likes to work at the court, and prefers not to take work home with her. Many of the justices do a lot of traveling, and they will bring many briefs with them. So, there are varied work habits among the nine.

GS: Now, I know that only a certain number of lawyers are qualified to present before the Supreme Court. How do they do that?

And are they rigorously timed during their presentations? I've heard that the justices can be very aggressive in their questioning, as well. Tell us about how it all works.

Biskupic: Each side of a given case traditionally gets thirty minutes to state its case, for a total of one hour. To argue before the court, you have to be party to the case, but you also have to be admitted to the Supreme Court Bar, which is actually fairly easy to get admitted to. You just have to have practiced in one of the state bars for a certain number of years. But the questioning from the justices is very rigorous, and the justices are more talkative and rapid-fire in their questioning.

GS: They can interject at anytime, as I am now.

Biskupic: Oh, my gosh; they run the show. They completely run the show. And sometimes an advocate can hardly get a sentence in before some justice has asked a question. And then what happens is you get the set time—thirty minutes—and when you only have five minutes left, a white light goes on at the lectern to warn the lawyer that his or her time is almost up, and then a red light pops on when your time is completely up. And the chief justice has cut people off mid-syllable. The timing is very rigorous.

GS: But that timing includes the questions that you are responding to from the justices, correct?

Biskupic: Yes, indeed. And here's another thing that a lot of people don't know: The justices will often suddenly argue with each other from the bench and use the poor man or woman at the lectern as a foil. They'll say things like, "Don't you think such and such?" Justice Antonin Scalia is wonderful at this—planting some argument with the lawyer, who he may believe isn't doing an effective enough job at something that Justice Scalia believes in, or ripping strips off him if it's something that he doesn't think is a legitimate argument.

There's so much talking going on, and people walk out of there exhausted. Lawyers have a really hard time.

GS: This must be the most dramatic show in town, when you think about it.

Biskupic: It's wonderful, because it's the main way that you can see these nine individuals that are deciding the law of the land. And it is the last stop. There is simply no higher authority to appeal to.

GS: I want to turn now to the individual justices. Let's start at the top with the chief justice, William Rehnquist. He was educated at Stanford and Harvard and was nominated to the court by President Nixon in 1971, and then nominated to be chief justice by President Reagan in 1986.

Biskupic: That's right. And he is 79 years old. He was a World War II veteran in the Army Air Forces, which I mention only because the topic of the day is national security. He's also a prolific author and has a knack for writing on subjects that end up being topical. He actually wrote about historic impeachments before the Clinton scandal and before he presided over the impeachment. And right now he's finishing up a book on the disputed Hayes-Tilden election of 1876, which he says he started before *Bush v. Gore*.

But I want to read you a quote from one of his other recent books that is very timely today. The book is called *All the Laws But One: Civil Liberties in Wartime*, published in 1998. He wrote, "It is neither desirable nor is it remotely likely that civil liberty will occupy as favorite a position in wartime as it does in peacetime. It is both desirable and likely that more careful attention will be paid by the courts to the basis for the government's claims and necessity for curtailing our civil liberties."

Thus, what he says is the laws will not be silent in time of war, but they will speak with a somewhat different voice—a somewhat more muted voice. So he has done some thinking in this area of civil liberties versus national security.

He has thought about retiring, but I don't think he would ever leave the bench if there wasn't a GOP president in the White House.[2]

GS: Fascinating. Now, John Paul Stevens took his seat in December 1975. I think of the chief justice as essentially a conservative sort of jurist. I tend to think of John Paul Stevens as a more liberal one. Am I right?

Biskupic: You are. He was appointed by Gerald Ford, a Republican president. But the way the court has shifted and the views that John Paul Stevens has had over the years have put him much more to the left on the court. So he's actually been somebody who's been very critical of some aggressive law enforcement policies from the executive branch, and somebody who's also been very critical of the court's emphasis on states' versus federal power.

I do want to mention that he was in the Navy and earned the Bronze Star. Shortly after September 11th, at a public gathering, he toasted George Bush as our commander-in-chief. So he comes from a lot of different attitudes on national security and civil liberties. He generally is one of our more liberal members, but I think that he's also very mindful of the importance of being able to fight internationally.

GS: The next jurist I want to discuss is an extraordinarily fascinating person and the subject of the book you're working on—Sandra Day O'Connor. She joined the court in September 1981,

---

2. Chief Justice Rehnquist died in 2005.

and my perception of her is that she's a highly sought-after swing vote on very crucial questions.

Biskupic: She runs the Supreme Court. She is not just the swing vote, George, she is the person who actually crafts the rationale. As I sometimes say, she's the man to see.

She doesn't like to say that, of course, and she's always dismissing the press reports about her influence, but I also think she likes it, because she's a politician at heart. She actually came up through Arizona as a state politician. She was not in the military, but she did have an unusual experience related to World War II. She grew up on a ranch right at the New Mexico and Arizona border, and one day when she was 15 years old, she saw part of the mushroom cloud from the atomic testing in nearby New Mexico. I find that fascinating, in that she's part of another era, even though, as a woman, she never had an opportunity to serve in the military.

But she's quite an influential justice and she's also very mindful of where public perception is.

GS: This all makes me mindful of the fact that these justices are so rooted in World War II and past realities of a time when our nation was also under threat. So they can relate today back to that, which is very interesting, I think.

Biskupic: That's right, and we happen to have just talked about the three eldest. Anthony Kennedy and Antonin Scalia are both sixty-seven and were appointed by Ronald Reagan. So, they're a touch younger and come at things a little differently, in terms of their historic sensibility. They both tend to be more conservative, especially Justice Scalia.

Kennedy is not as firm in terms of right-wing views. He's more conservative than, for example, David Souter or Stephen Breyer or Ruth Bader Ginsburg; but he's a swing vote. He's how you describe Sandra Day O'Connor, but he's not as critical in terms of gathering the majority to his point of view. He's more with the Rehnquist majority in terms of liking the diminishment of federal power and favoring states' rights.

Another thing I'd like to mention is that, after the September 11th terrorist attacks, he joined up with other leaders in the American Bar Association to start a program called "Dialogue on Freedom," designed to get students talking about civic values and other cultures—to open their minds more to diverse groups internationally and here at home. So he's another person who I think has done some serious thinking about what's going on in the world and some of the themes that we are now much more aware of because of September 11th.

GS: You know, my favorite Supreme Court stories involve the justices who do the unexpected and become something other than what people thought they might be. Earl Warren, for example, was quite a surprise to many.

Biskupic: Especially to President Eisenhower, who put him on the bench.

GS: Exactly. And wasn't it Justice Black who came from a kind of bigoted growing up to become a chief proponent of equal rights?

Biskupic: That's right. He had once been a member of the Ku Klux Klan in Alabama.

GS: It may not be as dramatic, but Justice Souter has been something of a surprise to those who appointed him, hasn't he?

Biskupic: David Souter is sixty-four and was appointed by the first President Bush in 1990. John Sununu, working for President Bush at the time, said, "Oh, he's a home run for conservatives." Well, he hasn't been. The new mantra from conservatives is, "Please, no more Souters!"

He is definitely on the left on the Supreme Court, although I should say that this Supreme Court is, overall, judicially conservative—especially compared with the court under Earl Warren. Souter is definitely someone who leans to the left and finds himself siding more with the Clinton appointees than the other Bush and Reagan appointees.

He's an interesting guy. He was born in Massachusetts and reared in New Hampshire, and he really is a Yankee. He keeps to himself. He enjoys reading. He eats alone at his desk—usually an apple and some yogurt. He's very charming, but he's not somebody whom you'll ever see out on the speaker circuit. If you do catch him, it's the one time for the year. On the bench, he often plays foil to Justice Scalia. They're very funny together sometimes—there's a lot of elbowing between the two up there on the bench.

GS: Our next justice, Clarence Thomas, seems to be very much to the right on the Court, and he was, of course, the subject of that extraordinary Senate hearing. He's also the youngest, isn't he?

Biskupic: He is. He's just fifty-five, and he was appointed by the first President Bush in 1991. The hearing you refer to is the one that exploded when Anita Hill, then a law professor at the University of Oklahoma, came forward and said that he had sexually harassed her when she was an employee of his. It was a nationally televised event. Everybody saw a "he said, she said" hearing, and obviously we will never know exactly what happened.

But he has remained very controversial because a lot of people remember that, and also because he is the only African American justice at this time and he consistently votes against programs that are arguably important to African American leaders—from affirmative action to majority-minority voting districts and voting rights.

Now, he does speak a lot. He speaks to a lot of conservative organizations, but also to a lot of student groups. He loves talking to students.

He also had a very rough upbringing. He grew up in Pinpoint, Georgia, and he had a rough time. His father walked out early on. He didn't have much growing up. Fortunately, as he compellingly recounted during his hearings, some Catholic nuns took him under their wing, and he eventually got a scholarship to Holy Cross, then wound up at Yale Law School, which somebody with his roots typically could not have done.

He ended up coming to Washington with a wave of conservatism. And Ronald Reagan put him at the Equal Employment Opportunity Commission. After that, he wound up on a very powerful Appeals Court at the District of Columbia Circuit. Then, of course, he was elevated to the Supreme Court by George H.W. Bush.

GS: Now, Ruth Bader Ginsburg. If Clarence Thomas is to the right, I guess people would say Ruth Bader Ginsburg is very much to the left. She was an appointee of President Clinton.

Biskupic: Correct. She was President Clinton's first appointee. She replaced Byron White in 1993. She really made a name for herself in her younger years as an advocate for women's rights at the American Civil Liberties Union. And she actually argued five or six cases before the Supreme Court on trying to get more protection under the Constitution for women under the Equal Protection Clause and was very successful. She often talks about how it's still hard for women to be recognized for their accomplishments, but that it will be less hard for her daughter's and granddaughter's generation.

She's very interesting. She loves opera and she says she always wanted to be a diva, but she had no voice. She told a group of students last year that it was probably to her advantage, because opera singers have to leave the stage by the time they're sixty or seventy, but Supreme Court justices can keep thinking and writing into their seventies, eighties, and even nineties.

GS: I'm not surprised. Now, turning to Stephen Breyer, who took his seat in 1994. By my account that makes him the youngest, in terms of service. What can you tell us about him?

Biskupic: Well, you know what happens when you're the most junior? You have to take notes during the conference. And you have to be the one who opens the door.

GS: Is that a tradition?

Biskupic: Yes. You actually have some freshman responsibilities at the court. And he's been a freshman longer than anyone else because this court has been together for ten years. It's the longest, most stable court in the history of our country.

So, he's been the one opening the door. The justices meet in a beautiful conference room with a wonderful oil painting of Justice John Marshall from the early 1800s on the wall over the fireplace. It's a wonderful room. But it's only the nine of them in there. No clerks or secretaries are allowed into this room. So, if the justices want some information from outside the room, they have to send a note out—and it's Justice Stephen Breyer who, as the most junior justice, has to give the note to the officer at the door. So it's a bit of a chore.

Just to give you a little bit more about his personality—he was actually born in San Francisco, but he's got strong ties to the Boston area. He was an Appeals Court judge up there, and then he taught at Harvard. He is a very pragmatic justice, and is always thinking about how a particular ruling will affect people on the streets.

GS: Before we conclude this marvelous conversation, I want to ask you if you think any of the justices will retire soon.

Biskupic: Well, you don't hear about it now because an election year is a very politically hot time to step down. But that said, I think that no matter who is elected in November, given the ages of these justices, we could probably see some retirements in 2005 or 2006.

Originally broadcast April 5, 2004.

16

James MacGregor Burns
From Transactional to
Transformational Leadership

*What makes a great and effective leader? Pulitzer Prize–winning
presidential biographer James MacGregor Burns has spent the
majority of his professional career thinking about this question in
relation to American political culture. Best known for his 1978 theory
of "transformational leadership," Burns continues to pioneer and
shape the area of leadership studies. In 1981 he helped establish the
Leadership Academy at the University of Maryland, which promotes
leadership, scholarship, and education, especially among those who
historically have been underrepresented in public life.*

※

George Seay: I want to go back in time to 1978 and your groundbreaking book *Leadership*.[1] You gave us a new vocabulary for
leadership in that book: *transactional* and *transformational*,
which we'll get to in a moment. But I think you did something
very early in that book which I found fundamental to everything
else, and that's to distinguish between the power wielder and the
leader. Would you remind us of what that distinction is?

---

1. James MacGregor Burns, *Leadership* (HarperCollins, 1978).

Burns: As the term indicates, a power wielder is a person who mainly rules through power, and there's a short word for that as compared to leader: the ruler. To me, the leader is somebody who obviously has to use power in governing a people, but he or she does it in terms of overriding values. I know we hear a lot about values, and it gets trivialized at times, but when I talk about values I mean the great values that inform a nation.

GS: Things that go to the soul of a people, perhaps.

Burns: Yes. Incidentally, no one has reached that as well as Woodrow Wilson, who understood what it is a leader really is willing to fight for, and to fight for those values and finally break through.

GS: When you speak of Woodrow Wilson in that way, I get the sense you're speaking especially of your notion of transforming leadership—of a president, in this case, who can look into the soul and history of a people and then elevate them. Is that right? And does he exemplify your idea of a transforming president in the twentieth century?

Burns: Exactly, except he failed in the end to do the thing that he most wanted to do, which was to have the United States join the League of Nations. But he tried so hard to do that. He fought for it and, in effect, he died for it—literally, and twenty years later, the memory of Wilson and his effort and what we failed to do was, I think, partly responsible for us taking the lead in setting up the United Nations.

GS: So, a transforming leader who fights the big battles can win, even posthumously, in a sense.

Burns: That's a good point, and absolutely right for many others besides Wilson.

GS: An important point I think you're also making is that a transforming leader is willing to fight those battles no matter the cost.

Burns: Yes, and willing to face conflict. So many politicians shrink from conflict. It's always impressive to see a man who stands up and says, "I believe in this and I'm going to fight for it."

GS: You outline in all your books that the willingness to face conflict, have convictions, and have courage are the essential components of transformational leadership. Those who shrink from conflict and lead on a lower level—is that the transactional level?

Burns: The transactional leader is the one we most often see. It's the leader, the politician, the businessman, the father, or the spouse, who makes deals, who negotiates, who reciprocates. They go through life, and this is a very crucial role in that way, transacting the business of the day, executing the give-and-take, and that is what most of us do, most of the time.

That's what most politicians do most of the time. But there comes a time in our own lives, and perhaps in the life of our community, but particularly in the life of a nation, when more is needed than simply making deals, making exchanges, and negotiating. You have to take a stand and fight for it, and if you're a successful transforming leader, then there are changes all through society as a result of the position you took.

GS: That certainly brings to mind George Washington, Abraham Lincoln, and FDR, but I would think you might agree with me that most of our leaders have been transactionalists.

Burns: Yes. First of all, because it's partly in the nature of the American people. We are negotiators, get-along, go-along people, which is good most of the time. But that's also true because it's very difficult to be a transforming leader. It's very dangerous. Again, we go back to Wilson, because it's rather interesting, looking back on this man who fought the great fight for what he believed in. Historians often refer to him as a failure.

He was not a failure. First of all, he was very effective in his early presidency; but again, he made the fight and making the fight is the first step in a great battle.

GS: How would you respond to someone who said to you, "Jim, this is all well and good. These great visionary leaders—these transformers—have been remarkable people, but can't that get a society into trouble? Aren't you better off with transactionalists, who just play the game, broker support, and get things done, but don't push us to the edge?"

Burns: My answer would be that yes, it is dangerous, but that's why I bring values into this so strongly. The great leaders have to be tested by a set system of values, and this nation has values.

I'm not talking about ethics and virtues, although those are important. I'm talking about the great values that guide a country, though a lot of people feel that's just talk. I did a three-volume work in American history investigating the extent to which American people have pursued a set of values through these two hundred or so years. Not only have they pursued a set of values, they have done a kind of prioritizing of values. It's easy to throw around these great words like freedom, equality, liberty, security, and so on. The important thing is what comes first, and the American people have made clear what comes first, and it's present in all the great documents: liberty.

So, getting back to your question, any president who violated the great elements of liberty would automatically, I hope, be rejected by the American people.

GS: By the same token, any president, such as Lincoln, who would take that notion and expand it, would be capable of visionary leadership and transform us.

Burns: That's absolutely right, and that's what happened with Lincoln. You know, he moved a lot during the Civil War, from being just a kind of transactional leader to being a transformer.

GS: That's an important point in itself. On the spectrum of transactional to transformational leadership, are there mid-points? Can a president, or any leader, act in more than one style, or combine them?

Burns: There are certainly combinations, and FDR is the classic case. I wrote a book called *Roosevelt: The Lion and the Fox*,[2] because that Machiavellian thought summarizes my view of Roosevelt, in that he was very much the transformational leader and he was very much the transactional leader. Of course, he had learned some lessons from Wilson, for whom he worked during World War I. Roosevelt skillfully combined those two qualities. There are degrees of transactional leadership. You can just be an absolute day-to-day broker, or you can use your transactional ability to bring about change. And there are degrees of transformational leadership as well.

---

2. James MacGregor Burns, *Roosevelt: The Lion and the Fox* (Harvest, 1956).

GS: This talk of presidents and lions and foxes and brokers and visionaries brings us to your current book, *Dead Center*, which you wrote with Georgia Sorenson.[3] It is a very detailed critique of the current president, Bill Clinton. You take him to task quite seriously for failing on the transformational scale.

Burns: That's true. I'd like to make that a little softer, because we rather admire his personal qualities. This is somewhat of a new approach, because usually people attack him for his personal failings, and like him as a politician.

We found him very impressive close up when we talked with him. In 1992, under very difficult circumstances because we were squeezed in a campaign car—not a limousine—Georgia Sorenson, myself, and Bill Clinton were practically sitting on top of each other. And it was a difficult moment in the campaign, one in which you could easily imagine him saying, "Why in the world do I have to spend time with these two scholars?" Instead, he was exceedingly pleasant, but most important, he was responding brilliantly to the questions we raised, which were questions about transformational leadership.

GS: So is the essence of your critique that this president, with all of his great personal qualities and political skill, was capable of a transformational leadership he well understood, but chose to act in a transactional manner too often?

Burns: Yes, and not only chose to, but in a sense he went to school in it, because he had been in, and a leader of, the Democratic Leadership Council, which preaches centrism. If you're a centrist, you're a transactional leader. That's what centrists do. And it was not just by chance that he followed that cause, that strategy; it was because he believed in it.

---

3. James MacGregor Burns and Georgia Jones Sorenson, *Dead Center: Clinton-Gore Leadership and the Perils of Moderation* (Scribner, 1999).

GS: What would you say if someone said to you, "That's well and good, but that's all he could get away with? That's all you could do in America at the close of the twentieth century—lead from the center, as a transactionalist."

Burns: I would say that, to a certain extent, that's true, because we have a constitutional system of checks and balances. You constantly have to negotiate with the House, the Senate, even the judges, and with the states.

But the greatness of the great presidents has been that they have risen above that. They've done their negotiating and so on, as in the case of Wilson, who was very skillful at that. But there comes a time when you have to rise above it. That was true of Abraham Lincoln. It was true of Wilson. It was true of Roosevelt, who was so frustrated by the checks and balances—the Supreme Court was striking down his legislation—that he took a much stronger position and tried to transform certain aspects of the American system. It's a dangerous game, George. There is no question about it.

GS: *Dead Center* talks about the perils of moderation. Where is the danger in transactional presidencies that don't become transformational ones?

Burns: The danger is that government doesn't make much progress. It does not change itself compared with the enormous changes that are taking place outside of government. We live in a time of relentless and titanic change in technology, science, business, entertainment, media, agriculture, war, and the like. And watching those changes as I do, as we all do, and looking at the feeble, slow effort of government to deal with those changes, indicates to me the need for very strong and vigorous leadership.

GS: In part, you seem to be talking about Bill Gates and those like him in the private sector—the private sector leadership that now has control of technology and wealth and is moving ahead faster than the government.

But in defense of the government, isn't it difficult to really get a sense of what all this means? Isn't it difficult to react transformationally at a point when we may not yet understand what we're faced with?

Burns: I don't think it's hard to understand the problems, and what worries me are two things. One is we have very little control over those changes outside of government. We do have some control over changes in government.

The other thing is that we don't solve our problems. I've lived a pretty long life, and from the beginning of the New Deal, when these problems were dramatized, until this morning's newspaper, these problems of health and jobs and housing and all the rest—such a well-known list—it's kind of boring to go through it.

GS: Would you include education on that list?

Burns: Of course—education above all. These go on and on, and they're deeply rooted in the structure. They're terribly hard to deal with, and only a strong push from inside government will ever help solve these problems.

GS: Bill Bradley ran a primary campaign that many thought was oriented to big ideas, and I think big ideas are at the essence of transformational leadership. As we know, he got nowhere with the voters. Is it, at some level, also a question of the appetite for change within the body politic—that there has to be an audience, if you will, for the transforming leadership that's ready to do it?

Burns: Yes, of course. And we live in good times, and we're complacent and happy, so it makes it very difficult for a politician to take a strong line. But some presidents have been able to do it.

The classic example is Theodore Roosevelt. He did not have a depression on his hands. He did not have a war. He had good times. He would have loved to have a war, but he didn't have a war as president. He brought about amazing changes through sheer leadership—intensity, conviction, continuity, follow-through, pushing, pushing, pushing. So he's given presidents an example of what you can do without a crisis.

GS: And what do you think Bill Clinton could have done with the unprecedented power and prosperity that we have had for the last eight years?

Burns: I simply think he could have taken a much stronger line ideologically, and a good example of this is the tax situation. He typically would deal with the tax situation in terms of balancing the budget. In my view, in terms of values, the great problem with our tax structure is the sheer inequity and unfairness of the tax system. Clinton is very good at protecting it. He vetoes the estate tax reduction, abolition, and so on, but he's not very good at rallying the people behind a moral issue, which is that of fairness and equality.

GS: Do you think he could have done that in the face of the conservative challenge he faced?

Burns: I think it would have made him much more successful if he had; if he had mobilized people behind his idea of equality, instead of just balancing the budget, even though it's nice to have a balanced budget.

GS: It seems that centrism, as a philosophy, is now the way of the West. You have Tony Blair in Britain, Gerhard Schroeder in Germany. Do you think this is a longstanding trend? The current election cycles suggest it might be.

Burns: It will be a longstanding thing until there's a real economic crisis, and that will be the test of a lot of what we're talking about here. I had one uncle who shot himself during the Great Depression, another who was traumatized and never worked again, and I can tell you many other stories about the actual impact of a depression on a family and a community. If we ever get into that kind of situation again, it will test a lot of what we're talking about here today.

GS: You recently have called for a commission on the presidency and what it might mean in the twenty-first century. To ask you somewhat critically: What would one more commission add to our understanding of this subject?

Burns: Let me give you an example of what a presidential commission or a national commission perhaps could do. Take the most frightening moment in my life, and yours, I expect—the Cuban Missile Crisis. For several days there was this continuing debate in the Kennedy Oval Office. It was not just Kennedy sitting there, pondering war or peace; it was a group of people struggling with this question. And I think because it was a collective decision of that sort, we came out the right way.

I would like to see a presidential commission just on foreign policy that's always there to advise the president. He or she would have to consult that commission and at least make this a collective decision, because the idea of one man with his finger on the trigger is something we cannot tolerate.

Originally broadcast October 30, 2000.

17

Seymour Martin Lipset

American Exceptionalism—How Different Are We?

Marty Lipset, long a senior scholar at the Wilson Center, is hard for me to characterize because I don't want to box in his talents. His work was groundbreaking, yet he always managed to sound like he was writing about a friend. Marty was one of the premier social scientists of the twentieth century. He wrote twenty books, beginning in 1950; his Political Man: The Social Bases of Politics *sold 400,000 copies and was translated into twenty languages.*[1] *This interview centers on* American Exceptionalism: A Double-Edged Sword, *published in 1996.*[2] *Marty died December 31, 2006.*

George Seay: Marty, early in your book you list some of the key qualities of American exceptionalism: beliefs in things like liberty, equality, individualism, populism, and laissez-faire government. I'm wondering if these beliefs amount to, in your opinion, a kind of a creed that binds us together the same way that ethnicity or religion might bind other peoples together.

1. Seymour Martin Lipset, *Political Man: The Social Bases of Politics* (Doubleday, 1960).
2. Seymour Martin Lipset, *American Exceptionalism: A Double-Edged Sword* (Norton, 1996).

Lipset: Yes. A number of people—and not just recently—writing about the United States have stressed that America is an ideologically creedal nation, and that it's organized around the concept of the good society, that Americanism, which is the term we use for the ideology, is an 'ism' just like liberalism, socialism, and communism are. It's, as I say, a sense of belief, and these beliefs stem back to the Declaration of Independence. Thomas Jefferson perhaps codified them or laid them down more than any other individual.

GS: Marty, listening to you I get the sense that one can say that a belief in Americanism is a kind of ideology in itself.

Lipset: It is. And as an ideological society, one which completed the first successful revolution for democracy, we put forth these doctrines and we welcomed people to join us. We were, and to some degree still are, a political party.

The way I put it is: Before 1917 and the Russian Revolution, Washington was Moscow, that is, it was the center of the world revolution. In the nineteenth century, democratic revolutionaries like Garibaldi of Italy or Sun Yat-sen of China would come to the U.S. for "R-and-R" or for money. After failing with some movement at home, they would come here to get more support, more money, and more enthusiasm, and Americans would give it to them because we regarded them as trying to make their homelands like the United States—democratic, egalitarian, and so forth.

GS: You know, implicit in what you're telling me, and one of the strengths of this country, is the way that we can bind the newcomer to the people who are already here because it's an acceptance of this belief, as opposed to race or creed.

Lipset: Other countries are historical countries. England, France, and Russia (not the Soviet Union) are all countries where people have a common history, common culture, and common language, but not a common value system or ideology.

In fact, I think there have only been two major ideological countries. One is the United States, which, of course, is happily still around. The other was the Soviet Union. Russia is a historical country, but the Soviet Union was an ideological country.

GS: Is it possible that this very quality of being a country based on an ideology, as we are, predisposes us to things like being a very moralistic country?

Lipset: I think it does. But in addition to the political creed, the idea of American exceptionalism comes from Alexis de Tocqueville. He first talked about the U.S. being an exceptional country in his great book *Democracy in America*, in which he pointed out in the 1830s that the United States was the most religious country in the world, and this is still true today. We have a myriad of public opinion poll data which show more Americans believe in God, heaven and hell, the devil, and so forth, than people in any other country in Christendom.

Tocqueville stressed the fact that American religion was different from that of Europe. The European religion is church religion—the Catholic Church, the Anglican Church, the Lutherans, and so on—very hierarchical institutions which are state-supported and state-related. American Protestantism is sectarian, which is largely congregational. The congregations determine who their ministers will be and insist that people study the Bible, so that moralism and individualism are both reinforced.

GS: I'm getting a sense of individualism, perhaps the roots of an anti-statist kind of mentality, that's very strong in our society. Do we see in these influences, and perhaps others, the roots of our very adversarial society? We seem to be constantly at litigation or contesting things.

Lipset: What you say is true. The litigation seems to stem from yet another aspect of our society, which is the Constitution and Bill of Rights. We are the first country, and to some extent the most important country, to have a constitution which dominates the politics of the country.

And of course, the Bill of Rights was filled with anti-state language. If you read the Bill of Rights, the language of it is largely, "Congress shall not pass a law which may do this or that." It's designed to restrict the government, not only against legislation, but to protect individuals when accused of crime, to guarantee fundamental rights such as free speech, so that Americans as individuals and as collective units, as states or organizations, go to court because there are these guarantees that the government may not do certain things.

An organization like the American Civil Liberties Union could not, and does not, exist in other countries because they don't have a Bill of Rights. Some of them are now beginning to adopt one. The Canadians adopted one in 1982. There's agitation in Britain to adopt one, but there still hasn't been one. I think the emphasis on having a Bill of Rights may help make us a very litigious country.

GS: Putting these various influences together—the constitutional roots, the religious experience, and so on—is that why, in this presidential election year, as we observe these campaigns and the conduct of American politics, both domestic and international, so much of it seems to be morally based? We seem to get in arguments that either demonize or exalt something. It's very unusual.

Lipset: This is again quite true, and I think it stems more or as much from the sectarian character of American religion. We're the only Christian country in the world where the overwhelming majority of the population are parishioners of the Protestant sects, as opposed to the churches. The Methodists, the Baptists and the hundreds of others are congregational, but also extremely moralistic and insistent that parishioners follow their own moral beliefs—not what the Pope, the king, or the government tells them, but what the Bible tells them as they interpret it, even if it means opposing the government.

So you find, for example, a very strong anti-war tradition in this country which dates way back. There was a scholar at the University of Chicago, Sol Tax, who did a study in the 1960s of the degree of anti-war activity. Vietnam was only rated fourth on the list. There was more anti-war activity in three other wars. During every single war, with the exception of World War II, when the attack on Pearl Harbor ended the debate, there has been a large-scale anti-war movement. Americans don't feel obligated to support a war if they think it's a wrong war.

Perhaps one of the most striking examples of this, which isn't widely known, was during the Mexican War. Thousands of American soldiers—including, according to the articles on the subject, West Point graduates—deserted and joined the Mexican Army because they thought that Mexico was right and we were wrong, and that they should be on the right side.

In the Civil War, you had people on both sides who didn't like what was going on. There were hundreds of thousands of conscientious objectors to World War I. We all know about Vietnam, but there was a lot of resistance to the Korean War, as well.

On the other side of the coin, it's not just the anti-war movements that are moralistic. We go to war for moral reasons. We always define the war in moral terms. When Ronald Reagan talked about the enemy, he called it the "Evil Empire"—satanic terms. He was being as American as apple pie.

GS: Help me understand something I've long wondered about. In terms of the classic definition of a liberal or conservative state, where do you place the United States?

Lipset: It depends. In terms of classic liberalism, which is anti-statism, the United States is the most liberal country. Friedrich Hayek, who is the great economic guru of people whom we now call conservatives—laissez-faire people—was furious if you ever called him a conservative. Conservatives in his native Austria were people who supported the king, feudalism, or the state church. He was for laissez-faire, a weak state.

Well, the United States is still the country with the weakest state. We're having debates now about the budget and the size of government and taxation. It might astonish Americans to know, and particularly some Republicans, that our deficit, in terms of the proportion of the gross national product, is the lowest in the developed world. Our tax rate is the lowest tax rate. The only country which comes close to us in low tax rates is Japan, and it taxes in other ways.

So, in fact, our taxes and our debts are low, not high, but Americans scream and think they're way too high. Part of the reaction of Americans to the deficit is that it's immoral to owe money and we have that kind of feeling about it. It becomes an aspect of morality.

GS: Are we libertarian, in that sense?

Lipset: We're not libertarian in the absolute sense. For example, we have more people in jail than any other country, and that's certainly not a libertarian practice. But if by *libertarian*, one means that we seek to put more constraints on power of the government, we're more libertarian than most other countries.

GS: Speaking of crime, you say in the book that an exaggerated individualism may be playing into some of this, but also the emphasis that we put on success, where ends often may be more important than the means.

Lipset: Here's an interesting way to look at it. Baseball's Leo Durocher once put it, "Nice guys finish last." Lord's Cricket Club in London has as its motto, "It matters not who wins the game. It matters how you play it." Well, for Americans it matters whether you win or not, and we place tremendous emphasis on upward mobility, success, and achievement.

This creates a situation where if you succeed, that's well and good, but if you don't succeed, you're cast as a failure and you feel yourself a failure more strongly than people do in societies which have a more overt class system, as most of the European countries do.

And, one way to react to being a failure is, if you can't win by legitimate means, you may try to win by illegitimate means. By hook or by crook—a lot of Americans will try it by crook.

GS: Does this kind of thing in another way influence our attitudes toward the poor—that they're somehow not deserving?

Lipset: I think it does, because we assume that everybody should try to succeed and has a chance to succeed. One way we do spend more money than other countries is on education, because education is seen as a path to mobility. We don't spend money on helping the poor, except to succeed.

Americans believe in equality of opportunity, not condition. Equality of condition would mean that you give everybody the same amount through some kind of handout—an entitlement system. The emphasis on equality of opportunity creates the perception that it's a race for success.

GS: It's somewhat of a dilemma as to why a country constructed like ours has not resulted in the formation of a socialist party. Why is that?

Lipset: I think there are a number of reasons, but one of them, as we've already discussed, is that we're strongly anti-statist. We think the strong state is bad, so I would say that Americans are more likely to be anarchist than socialist.

Another problem is that our political system, with its focus on electing one person as president rather than members of parliament, makes it very difficult to get a third party. We've had a number of third party candidates. Ross Perot in 1992 was the most recent, and he received 19 percent of the vote. George Wallace got 12 percent in 1968. Robert La Follette got 17 or 18 percent in 1924. So, Americans have been willing to vote for protest candidates, but no socialist has ever gotten more than 6 percent, and that was Gene Debs in 1912. Except for that election, the socialist vote was usually 2 percent or less. Americans will vote protest, but not socialist.

GS: You've also pointed out that in the minds of many Americans, our capitalism produces the benefits of socialism.

Lipset: There have been a number of writers, including some who were socialists, who have argued that the social relationships and values of the economic ownership system of this country have been very much the same as those which socialists want—namely, equality of status, equality of relationships, and freedom and the like.

A man named Leon Sampson, a left-wing socialist, in 1933 wrote a book called *Toward a United Front* (Farrar & Rinehart), in which, to demonstrate his point, he had on one side of the page statements from leading Americans, and on the other side statements by Marx, Engels, Lenin, and Stalin. And they're almost identical.

If I were to ask you who you thought the Americans were, you might say Lincoln or Jefferson, or the like. They actually were Herbert Hoover, Andrew Mellon, and John D. Rockefeller. The descriptions from these strong believers in American capitalism of the good society, their comments on abolishing poverty, creating equal opportunity and equal status and so on were very similar to those of the socialists.

GS: I want to turn now to your treatment in the book of what you call "outliers." I don't mean just America as opposed to other countries, but within our society, you point out, we have out-liers. African Americans, for example. The point that you make is that through the roughly 350-year-history of slavery and seg-regation, African Americans have been forged into a caste. That is a word that is very unusual in the American lexicon, and you say that this has really affected their experience and complicated their adherence to the creed and their participation in it. Is that right?

Lipset: I think this is true. By *caste*, one means units of stratifica-tion in which there is no mobility, in which people are born into a system and stay there, and people who are higher do not expect them to try to move into their position. So it's a caste, not a class system, and anyone who was partially black was classified as black. There was no mobility. African Americans were the lower caste and at first not allowed to have any of the higher positions.

Since the sixties, we've changed a great deal and there has been an enormous improvement in a number of aspects of the situation of African Americans. But it's still far from equality.

In fact, one of the striking things is intermarriage. Among whites, the melting pot is working like it never has before, and there is a tremendous amount of intermarriage. Most Jews marry non-Jews. Most Catholics marry non-Catholics. Even 40 percent of Chicanos born in this country marry non-Chicanos. The over-whelming majority of Italians, Irish, and Japanese marry people of another extraction.

But with blacks, it's something like 2 to 3 percent. Whites don't marry blacks and blacks don't marry whites, so at that level too, we have a caste system. And while there's been enormous improvement in economic opportunities and political rights for blacks, it still hasn't brought blacks and whites together and there is still a lot of segregation. In fact, the efforts of integration which many whites accepted and many black leaders pushed for have sort of moved backward. A lot of blacks no longer want integration, but rather want to get more for themselves as a separate group.

GS: Marty, bring what you said to help us understand the division of opinion on a subject as hot and controversial as affirmative action. Does this caste history, for example, predispose African Americans to look at their interest in this subject in a way that whites don't see, or vice versa?

Lipset: Interestingly, if you look at poll data, while most whites are against affirmative action quotas or preferences, a surprisingly large percentage of blacks, often close to 50 percent, oppose it as well. And part of this is that the American emphasis has been on individualism, meritocracy for the individual and not the group, so that the best people should be motivated to try to rise, and the best people should rise through education or in other ways.

GS: In the book, you hint at what might be a different approach to this. You point out that the underclass, which gets a great deal of attention in our society, is really something of a residual—it's numerically a problematic group, but not a large one—and that if you focused on the similarity of problems in the inner cities and places like Appalachia, you might find the same set of problems. That, then, would argue for designing an affirmative action policy that would be aimed at people in those conditions, no matter their race or location.

Lipset: The words *affirmative action* by themselves don't mean quotas. They mean that you do something for the group, and in fact, you find that if you ask people—whites or blacks—whether they favor *affirmative action* to make up for past discrimination, most people say yes. But if you say *affirmative action quotas*, you get a different response.

Ideally, you spend a lot of money to, in Lyndon Johnson's terms, bring them up to the start of the race equally, but not to determine the outcome of the race. The question then, of course, is what it takes to do that, because, unfortunately, a lot of the educational research suggests that you have to start pretty young. By the time the kids are five and six, it's already too late if they've had a bad family background and bad conditions. You really have to begin with one- and two-year olds, not five- and six-year olds.

GS: Another outlier group that you treat in the book is the American Jewish community. American Jews account for only 2.5 percent of the population, which I think might surprise many people, and yet as small as it is, they have attained in their history here what can only be called extraordinary levels of professional intellectual achievement. The record is one of enormous and impressive success. What's interesting, though, is that it's a community that, by and large, has stuck to its political liberalism even as other groups gaining affluence have not. Why?

Lipset: There are a number of reasons. One is the memory of history. Most American Jews came here from Eastern Europe around the time of World War I, when they were being totally discriminated against. They were in the situation like the blacks here, or worse legally, and in that context, they could not be conservatives. In Czarist Russia, for example, where a lot of them had come from Poland, they were revolutionaries. If they were political, they supported the socialist movements, and many of the first generation Jews in this country belonged to socialist groups. The largest socialist paper in the United States was the *Jewish Daily Forward*, which was in Yiddish and had a couple hundred thousand in circulation. So you have a continuation, a sort of family tradition, of being on the left and being for equality and the like.

The other thing is that, in terms of the historic memory of the Jews, which was strengthened by the worst experience in their history, the Holocaust, they've regarded the dominant host community of the Christians as anti-Semitic, especially the richer and more conservative Christians.

And even here, where Jews have done, as you said, incredibly well, if you poll American Jews about anti-Semitism, three-quarters of them will say it is a serious problem in the United States. If you then ask them if they personally have had any anti-Semitic experiences, most of them haven't. But this folk memory is a memory of anti-Semitism. And they often identify it with the right, because the liberals and the left were for equality and for bringing them into the system. They see the conservatives as the people who were anti-Semitic.

There's a more recent factor, as well, which is that of separation of church and state. As a minority, Jews have always been for separation of church and state. They don't want their children exposed to teachings which violate their beliefs. They like the idea of voluntary religion. Recent efforts to bring religion into the school system are something which Jews find very offensive.

If you look at polls among Jews, you find that a lot of the more well-to-do Jews have become more conservative on economic issues. But what keeps them Democratic and liberal are these social issues. They don't want religion in their schools and the Christian Coalition is something that scares them.

In spite of being probably the most well-to-do group, the Jews remain politically liberal. Somebody once put it that Jews earn like Episcopalians and vote like Hispanics. Somebody else said they vote like blacks, but that's not quite true because only 10 percent of blacks vote Republican, whereas 20 to 25 percent of Jews do. So their division is more like Hispanics than it is like blacks.

Originally broadcast July 22, 1996.

PART III

Thinkers, Poets, and Playwrights

18

Walter Reich

The Mechanisms of Evil

For Walter Reich, the question of evil among human beings is very personal, starting with the Holocaust. Born into hiding in wartime Poland, Walter spent his early years in a displaced person's camp in Berlin before coming to the United States when he was three years old. He has studied Soviet abuse of psychiatry, the Israeli-Palestinian conflict, terrorism, human rights, and medical ethics. Yet I believe firmly that Walter remains optimistic that we, as people, can do better. He is a professor at George Washington University in psychiatry, international affairs, and ethics. He has also been director of the U.S. Holocaust Memorial Museum.

✳

George Seay: Walter, the subject of evil is grim, but I can't imagine a better person to talk about it with. You might call this conversation a discussion of the evil in every man, because we're going to talk about what makes otherwise good people do obviously evil things.

Let me start by asking you about the importance of the sanction of authority. How important is it to have someone at the top of an organization saying, "You are permitted to act in this way."

Reich: It's incredibly important—not only to organizations, but for individuals as well, because it's one of the sanctions that permits people to disengage from the moral precepts that ordinarily govern their behavior. There are a number of mechanisms that one can identify that make it possible for somebody to do something that he or she would normally consider to be an odious act. And those mechanisms account for much of the ability of people who are proud of their home lives, who have nice families, who are kind to their pets, and so on, to do evil things. There's an old grim joke about Hitler having been kind to his dog and a nice vegetarian, but of course, we also know what else Hitler did.

GS: We certainly do. I gather from you that one has to—to use your word here—disengage; to become, in a sense, another person. Explain what you mean by that.

Reich: You find or put yourself in a situation that enables you to do something you would not ordinarily do. The issue of self-deception—fooling yourself about what it is you're doing—is a very complicated one. It's philosophically problematic because the only way in which one can explain self-deception is to assume there are two people somehow, or two halves. There's a conscious and an unconscious part of a person, and that one part deceives the other part.

Philosophically, that's a problem. How can you say that you don't know what you're doing when you really know what you're doing?

There are a number of mechanisms people employ, such as

the one you mentioned—appeals to authority. "I was just carrying out orders," was a common defense from the Nuremberg
trials. There are several others, as well. For example, there is something that has been called cognitive reconstrual, a reconstruction
of a situation so that one convinces oneself in some fashion that
the people who are being harmed are actually evil themselves
and deserve it.

GS: This makes me very curious about the environment in which
it happens—the seed bed, if you will, for this. And the word
which comes to my somewhat untutored mind is paranoia. Is
there some kind of massive paranoia or altered way of looking
at things that society has to be in for this to be operative?

Reich: There are certainly circumstances that affect processes like
this taking place. They don't all occur in all of the places where
these evil acts unfold. Certainly, if people are experiencing hardship and times are not good, there is a greater likelihood of a
populace trying to identify the cause of its misfortune.
   If things are rough—whether it's Germany or contemporary
Russia—it increases the likelihood that anti-democratic and fas-
cist forces that identify a particular cause, or group, or force, or
power, or foreign element, or something, will be embraced. Those
elements are cast as the cause of the misfortune that the people
are experiencing, and they are encouraged to somehow resist or
fight against that element, or to rid their society of it entirely.

GS: So it's the climate that allows the demagogue to do his work.

Reich: It's like a fertilizer. It enables the demagogue to flourish.

GS: One of the most frightening things about this entire phenomenon is that it can take place in a Third World society, like
Rwanda, but it can also take place in the most sophisticated and
developed of societies. That's astounding, in a way.

Reich: You're right. It is astounding. And one of the reasons that the Holocaust was so very astounding, of course, was that it took place in the heart of Europe, within a society that was, in many respects—certainly in music, literature, and art—among the most civilized, by usual definitions of that term, in the world. Maybe the most civilized, in some fashion. And yet, it didn't take much, or it certainly didn't seem to take all that much, to get that society to focus itself into a ferocious act of evil.

GS: We've now had a half-century to examine the Holocaust, and can evaluate with hindsight the accounts of the perpetrators of these evil acts. What do they say, and how do you analyze it as a psychiatrist? Is there some generic way that the perpetrators came to grips with what they were doing and explained it to themselves or to others?

Reich: There was an illuminating study of a particular battalion, Battalion 101 of the German order police.[1] There is a widespread notion that all of what happened in the Holocaust was carried out by SS officers—a special group of evil men, almost as if they had a big 'E' on their foreheads, walking around saying, "We're evil."

Well, nobody says, or believes, that they're evil. That's something I want to get back to. Nobody thinks of themselves as evil. Hitler didn't think of himself as evil. Stalin, who was responsible for many millions of deaths, didn't either. There are all kinds of mechanisms people create to convince themselves of the fact that they're not evil.

In this particular battalion, many were order police that were not SS officers. Some were bookkeepers or pharmacists before the war, but they got into these order police battalions. They were put into them because they were too old for the regular army.

---

1. Christopher R. Browning, *Ordinary Men: Reserve Police Battalion 101 and the Final Solution in Poland* (HarperCollins, 1992).

Some of them were police officers in various towns. Some had no police background.

This battalion of about 500 men who were in their thirties, forties, or even a few in their fifties was sent into Poland, and during their time there, these men were responsible for the deaths of 83,000 Jews.

GS: These men killed 83,000 people?

Reich: Right. They either did it directly—they shot some 40,000 Jews in the head or back of the neck—and some 40,000 they stuffed into railroad cars that ultimately ended up in death camps, where they were gassed.

And what was really striking about the study was that it showed that at first many of the men found the killing unpleasant, even odious. When they would round up the Jews in various towns, they would take them one by one into the woods and just shoot them, and there were gory descriptions of the police officers from this battalion coming back with pieces of the brains and skulls of these Jews on their clothing, and some of them got sick. But, gradually, they got used to it. After the war, when they went on trial, most of them claimed they were among the nonshooters, but probably many more claimed not to have shot than actually did shoot.

GS: I want to turn to the individual aspect of this and what you said about people doing evil things and yet not admitting to themselves that they are doing it. How do you explain that as a psychiatrist? Why does that happen?

Reich: First of all, let me try to define what I mean by evil. I remember participating in a conference focusing on the Holocaust and individual motivations, and nobody used the word evil. All the participants were academics—historians, sociologists, or social scientists. I happened to be the commentator for that session, and I said that I think we can't help but use the word evil. One of the panel members was himself a Holocaust survivor and a historian, and said, "Well, you know it's usually seen as a theological word, and therefore we don't use it."

But we do use it in everyday life, and I don't necessarily define it in theological terms. I define it in practical terms, and my definition has something to do with an act or process, the result of which is the deliberate bringing of harm to other persons who are innocent of any intent to bring oneself harm.

I want to read something to you, if I may, because I just came across it today. I was looking at a book by Fred Katz called *Ordinary People and Extraordinary Evil*, which was published last year.[2] He uses in the beginning of the book two quotations that I think really are valuable in connection with what we're discussing.

One is from Aleksandr Solzhenitsyn, who of course is the great chronicler of the Soviet gulag—the system of prisoner camps under Stalin. In *The Gulag Archipelago*, he writes: "If only it were all so simple! If only there were evil people somewhere committing evil deeds, and it were necessary only to separate them from the rest of us and destroy them. But the line dividing good and evil cuts through the heart of every human being. And who is willing to destroy a piece of his own heart?"

And the second quotation is from Primo Levi, an Italian chemist who recently committed suicide. He was one of the chroniclers of Auschwitz—a Jew who was incarcerated and survived Auschwitz and wrote several books on his experiences. In *Survival in Auschwitz*, he writes: "Monsters exist, but they are too few in number to be truly dangerous. More dangerous are the common man, the functionaries ready to believe and to act without asking questions."

---

2. Fred Emil Katz, *Ordinary People and Extraordinary Evil: A Report on the Beguilings of Evil* (State University of New York Press, 1993).

GS: It's a rather uncomfortable moment to realize that what we are saying in this conversation is that we are all capable of acts of evil. No one is above it.

Reich: We are all, to a greater or lesser extent, capable of doing evil. There are some people who are more capable than other people. But we all have basic mechanisms that enable us to do bad things to other people and which apply in most cases of doing evil. We've already discussed the situation in which we cast the people to whom we want to bring harm as evil themselves, and deserving of the harm, and blame them for having hurt us—that it's a social benefit to hurt them and get rid of them.

Another mechanism has been called euphemistic labeling, in which one doesn't talk about what one is doing in its real terms and real descriptions. One uses euphemisms which are kind of a code to cover up.

GS: For instance?

Reich: Well, for example, in Auschwitz, bodies were called logs sometimes. So the order would be given to get rid of the logs.

There's yet another mechanism that people employ called displacement of responsibility, which we referred to before in terms of referring to authority. People say, "We're just following orders. It's not my responsibility. It's somebody else's."

There's also something that has been referred to as diffusion of responsibility. If you create a bureaucratic process in which everybody has only a small role, then nobody has to feel that they are personally responsible for the whole thing.

GS: The process did it.

Reich: The process did it. Auschwitz did it. Well, in reality there were individual acts in which people shot other people, or people dumped pellets of poison gas into the gas chambers; and in the end, they knew they were killing and they used other mechanisms to justify that.

There is also a mechanism of distortion of consequences, that is, convincing oneself that one isn't really hurting or bringing harm to somebody. For example, the idea of dropping a bomb on people who are thousands of feet below is easier than shooting a person in the neck, because it's anonymous.

In the famous experiments by Stanley Milgram at Yale, participants were ordered to give what they thought were electric shocks to other people.[3] More often than not, people obeyed the orders, even though they could hear what they thought were real screams of pain from those they were supposedly shocking. Some of the people quit, but many of them kept on applying more and more current, or thought that they were. Nobody actually got shocked in the experiment, but the participants didn't know that.

The participants would be told, "Well, you're not really hurting him much." And they would seize upon that as justification for being able to do it, even though many of them became extremely uncomfortable.

GS: To conclude, I want to ask how a society like ours builds barriers against this happening? Are there steps that you take that you're conscious of, in terms of things like human rights, which can make this less likely, rather than more likely, to occur?

Reich: I'm a child of what I consider, or hope, to be an age of reason. Maybe it's a self-deceptive fantasy, but I have the belief that we can learn from experience. I don't mean that it obviates a future similar experience, but that having experienced something terrible, we can learn from it about ourselves and about our societies.

---

3. See Stanley Milgram, *Obedience to Authority: An Experimental View* (HarperCollins, 1974).

One of the reasons I feel we're extremely fortunate in having in our midst here in Washington, and in America, this new Holocaust Museum, is that we decided as a country to give a place for an institution that dealt with something very terrible. And by its very existence—through its permanent exhibit and through its programs and research—we're shown what human beings are capable of. We won't all draw the same lessons from it, but I think we, in general, will conclude that human beings are capable of the most terrible things, and they're capable of those things as a result of the mechanisms that we were talking about. We have to watch what we do and how we think, and recognize in ourselves and in our societies inclinations and processes that can result in these kinds of terrible acts that we're referring to as evil.

I want to stress just one more thing. The museum, in its early section in its permanent exhibit, focuses on the dissolution of democratic institutions in Nazi Germany and the subsequent processes that resulted in the Holocaust. I think there's a very powerful cautionary tale that's particularly compelling and resonant for Americans, because Americans visit this city of Washington and go to the Lincoln Memorial and Washington Monument and Jefferson Memorial and often don't really appreciate what they have here, don't really understand that democracy is what stands between them and terrible things. And I think institutions like the Holocaust Museum can help orient a visitor to Washington, so that he or she understands what the value of democracy is and that we shouldn't take these things for granted.

Originally broadcast April 22, 2002.

19

Edward P. Jones
Unlocking the Complexities of Slavery

As a student at the College of the Holy Cross in the early 1970s, Edward P. Jones discovered the uncomfortable fact that there had been free black people who owned slaves in the antebellum South. "It was a shock that there were black people who would take part in a system like that," he later observed. "Why didn't they know better?" Jones ruminated on this question for more than 20 years, and it eventually served as the premise for his first novel, The Known World, *which won the 2004 Pulitzer Prize for Fiction and the 2005 International IMPAC Dublin Literary Award.*[1]

✳

George Seay: I want to begin by asking, for those of us who love books, why it is that you write? I've had the pleasure of reading other things you've written besides *The Known World*, and in a piece called "We Tell Stories," I got the impression that you don't have any choice but to write.

Jones: I think that's true. I think that, generally, writers fall into two categories—those who do it because one day they want to be another John Grisham and be wealthy and famous and all

---

1. Edward P. Jones, *The Known World* (HarperCollins, 2003).

that, and then there are people who do it because they are compelled to. They have no choice. And no matter where they are, they find themselves writing, whether physically on a page or in their heads, as has often happened with me over the years.

GS: I want to talk about that. In my mind, that's one of the most fascinating parts about how you write—that so much is done in your head. Can I take it from what you've just said, that it's a vocation, something one is born to, from which there is no escaping?

Jones: Yes. I think it's rather like, you know, something like a songbird. A songbird sings, and unless you do something to it, it's going to sing on, no matter what, and I think that's the case with me.

I did all the work on the book, and my hope was that somewhere at the end of the line someone would purchase it, but I didn't know that. That wasn't a guarantee. All I knew was I wanted to write it, I had to write it, and that's what happened.

GS: It was also interesting for me to learn that, after you received a number of extraordinarily prestigious awards for the book, your reaction was, "Well, I've got to get up and write tomorrow, too. These awards don't mean a thing about tomorrow."

Jones: No matter what they give you, no matter what they say about you, it doesn't help with the next chapter or the next story. You can't prop up an award on top of the computer and say, "Things: write." You have to do it yourself. You have to start back at the bottom of the mountain again, and nothing ever helps you to do that but whatever you have inside you.

GS: And in doing this you exercise an extraordinarily powerful degree of imagination that helps all of us visit a world that we otherwise would not have known very well. And I guess that's my next question for you. This use of imagination that began with a kernel of an idea and, in some sense, germinated and grew into *The Known World*, where did it begin with you?

Jones: It's so hard to answer that now, and when people ask me that kind of question I sometimes think that if I'd known that it would be received the way it has been received, I would have taken notes every day and kept a diary.

Seriously, though, I don't know. Probably the very first image I had may have been of Henry Townsend, a black man, on his death bed. And when he dies, he leaves about thirty-three slaves and a substantial portion of land to his widow. That image of Henry dying in a room with two or three women may have been the very first image I had. And then I had to create a world around that room and that house and that piece of land that he was on. That's pretty much where it started.

GS: Was the very idea of black slave ownership a starting point for you as well?

Jones: I was quite surprised to learn that there were black slave owners when I was in college. It wasn't a book; I think it was just some line some place, a footnote perhaps. Or something that a professor said in passing. And I just took it and sort of tucked it away in my head and didn't think about it again for any real reason for a long time, until I had finished the first book I wrote and was thinking about what I should do next.

GS: When Henry Townsend, the protagonist in this book, appeared to you, dying in that room—that image and vision grew over a decade, didn't it? I'm so fascinated by how so much of this was written in your head for a long time before you even sat down to put it on paper.

Jones: I think I started thinking about this in 1991–92. That's when so much began to come to me, starting with Henry's dying. And because it was the nineteenth century, it was slavery, and there was a great deal that I knew very little about, I had some forty or so books that I intended to read. I was going to read all of those books in a year or two, and then sit down to start writing.

But I kept putting off all the reading. I kept rebelling against doing all the research. So I kept putting it off, year after year. In the meantime, of course, the creative part of the brain continued to do what it has to do, and so the novel kept building and building in my head, even as I put off all the research.

In addition to reading all the books, I intended to visit a friend of mine in Lynchburg, Virginia, and use his county as a setting. Well, I never got around to visiting, but again, the years went on and I continued to create this book in my head.

There came a time when I needed to see the words on the page, and when I finally did sit down to write the entire book after about ten years, in 2001, I had twelve pages total. I had six pages of the first chapter and six pages of the final chapter. I didn't want to go any further than that because I was still thinking I had to do the research. I was still thinking I had to visit my friend to get the lay of the land.

And in 2001, I had five weeks of vacation from the day job I had at that time, and I told myself that I'd start reading in earnest. And again this thing in me just rebelled against reading all of those books. The book was in my head and I just sat down and started writing.

As for visiting my friend to get the lay of the land, I finally decided that I knew a little about this and a little about that and that I should just make up my own county. In the end, it worked well, because had I used his county I would have been confined and forced to limit myself to the history of that place. I couldn't have gone outside of that. If I had written a wrong sentence, someone would have called me on it. But you create your own world and you can say whatever it is you want to say about it.

GS: I want to read a sentence from the book to you and hear your thoughts on it. It's a question that might have haunted you as you wrote it: "What is it like for a people to become invisible in a country that the world sees as offering hope and promises to so many others?"

For those who are really concerned about the place of slavery in our history, that seems to me like a very powerful evocation of what its cost was.

Jones: It's always this great irony with this country, given the principles on which it was founded, the way so many people have not lived up to those principles over the centuries. They speak on one side of their mouth and then turn around and do something entirely contrary to what they just said.

GS: You know, in reading the book, there's a degree of quietness about your language and narrative. Is that a conscious choice?

Jones: Yes it is. It's like the Bible—I had a chance in graduate school to read the Bible and I was fascinated by the stories that I encountered, as well as the quiet language in which many of them were told.

But mainly, I knew that the situation of slavery brings with it its own emotion and I didn't need to add any more than that. I knew that I just needed to tell the story in a newspaper sort of fashion—these are the facts, this is what happened—and I didn't feel any need to layer any more emotion on top of any of that.

I often use the example of something that happened here in

Washington several years ago. A woman took her child to the supermarket to get ice cream, lost control of her car, and killed the child. I always remember that because I tell people that if you were writing a story about that situation, this woman, and her loss, the emotion of losing a child is there already. You don't need to say anything more than what happened. On a simple, plain day this woman goes out to do what millions of parents do every day and this horrible thing happened to her.

GS: And it speaks for itself.

Jones: It does, it does. And so much of what human beings go through has its own emotion and empathy. I don't like to use what I often call "neon" language. It's just not me. I'm sort of an understated guy to begin with, so it wouldn't work for me. You can go through my work and you would be hard pressed to find an exclamation point.

GS: Speaking of this empathy for human beings and letting their emotions come through naturally, that moves me to the next point I want to raise. There are so many different characters in this book, including freed blacks, enslaved blacks, white masters, poor whites, Indians—the entire population of Manchester County, Virginia, at that time. This is a difficult question to phrase, but here's the sense of it. Reading all of this and thinking about what's going on in the book, I got the impression that at least one moral lesson was that in a world that's constructed on evil, no matter what path people take, no one is unscathed by it. Everyone is affected.

Jones: Even the good people are often pulled into it, and the best thing that you can do is try to keep your bearings about you. One of the things I realized once I had finished the book was, without even thinking about it, the people who did not limit themselves to the known world, who saw a bit beyond what was in front of them—those are the people who could survive.

There's a slave named Elias who wants nothing more than to be free, and he takes many chances to try to escape until finally he can't do it anymore. And without even knowing it, he falls in love with this woman who is crippled and who can't possibly run away. And what he finds in caring for this woman and in marrying her and having children with her is a kind of peace and freedom that he hadn't realized that he could have while being enslaved. And I felt he was able to achieve this because he didn't limit himself to the world that he was given. Contrast that with the overseer in that plantation, Moses, a black man who has limited himself in so many ways that it eventually becomes his downfall.

GS: As we read any book, we try to apply it to our own lives, and from what you've just said, I'm getting a notion that it's the dreamers who hold the future because they can live beyond whatever their known world is.

And I want to ask you now about the complexities and moral ambiguities that arise in the known world. Are these complications confined to antebellum Virginia, or do the statements of this book have resonance in our own time, as well? Do they apply to our own known world—the same stratifications of race, caste, color, the same perversions of behavior against the constructs of what we call, or what we should call, our known world?

Jones: I think so. And I think part of the problem is that America has innumerable good points about it. I mean, I'm sitting here today. Had I been born someplace else, in another country, I'm not sure that I would be sitting here talking to you. But at the same time, this isn't a country that likes to stand still and question things too much. And I think that's how we emerged from the Civil War. We were happy that we survived it, but we didn't sit down and ask ourselves how we got into this situation and how we can improve things so that in fifty or a hundred years we don't have the problems that we had. This country has always been on the move and it's always been too busy to sit down and think things out.

GS: I want to get into some of the wonderful characterizations in the book. I would love it if you would read for us a passage that concerns two of the central characters of the book, William Robbins the slave master, and Henry Townsend, the former slave of Robbins and now a slave owner himself.

Jones: William Robbins once upon a time owned Henry's father and mother. And Henry's father, Augustus, eventually bought himself out of freedom, then bought his wife out of freedom, and then the two of them together bought the freedom of Henry.

At this point in the story, Henry has become a sort of protégé of William Robbins because he had spent so many years without his parents and under the guidance of William Robbins. So in a sense, Robbins has become like his father. This is years and years after Henry's mother and father had bought his freedom and Henry has become sort of well-to-do. He'd done very well for himself making boots and shoes and now he is building himself a house, and to help in building that house he has bought a slave, Moses, from William Robbins. This being Henry's first slave, he doesn't really know how to act. I think we should just say it that way. And so one day after he and Moses have been working on the house, they stop and they start wrestling, and William Robbins rides up and finds them and he calls Henry aside.

"Henry," Robbins said, looking not at him but out to the other side of the road, "the law will protect you as a master to your slave, and it will not flinch when it protects you. That protection lasts from here"—and he pointed to an imaginary place in the road—"all the way to the death of that property"—

and he pointed to a place a few feet from the first place. "But the law expects you to know what is master, and what is slave. And it does not matter if you are not much more darker than your slave. The law is blind to that. You are the master and that is all the law wants to know. The law will come to you and stand behind you. But if you roll around and be a playmate to your property, and your property turns around and bites you, the law will come to you still, but it will not come with the full heart and all the deliberate speed that you will need. You will have failed in your part of the bargain. You will have pointed to the line that separates you from your property and told your property that the line does not matter. . . . You are rollin' around now, today, with property you have a slip of paper on. How will you act when you have ten slips of paper, fifty slips of paper? How will you act, Henry, when you have a hundred slips of paper? Will you still be rollin' in the dirt with them?"

GS: Now, that is what the institution of slavery is going to demand of Henry despite Henry's intentions—I think at one point Henry even said that he's going to be a better master, a good master, and clearly that's not going to be.

Jones: Right. It's rather like saying, "Well, the old devil is dead. I'm the new devil and I'm going to be the best devil in hell that I possibly can." It's an impossibility.

GS: Before we conclude this discussion, I want to ask you how you teach. Again, going back to the powerful use of your imagination and creativity, how do you convey that to your students?

Jones: You can't. The only thing you can do is have someone write and then sit down with them and approach what they've written with all that you have learned in your life. There's no way that you can sit down and teach it. You can only give some sort of guidance.

"Well, you know, on this page the plot seems to go a little flat."

"This dialogue needs to be sharpened up."

"The whole climatic moment here isn't quite believable."

"Here's what I suggest."

And I do. I tend to suggest a lot.

GS: But the voice and the thought have to be theirs.

Jones: Right. I never assign any text when I teach because I feel if people want to be writers, they should already be reading anyway and they should not have to come to a class for me to tell them that.

GS: As we conclude, I think it's almost an inevitable question, and those of us who love novels really probably know why, but I want to ask the novelist—why is this novel important?

Jones: We're born into this world and what a novel does—whether you're reading about some coal miner in France in the nineteenth century or the wife of some doctor in one of Chekhov's stories—is it tells us that we're not alone in some way. You can be locked away in a jail cell and you can read about these people and realize that you are small, but in another way you are also big because there are other people who are suffering the same thing that you're suffering. Or they're being happy about the things that you're happy about.

I think the thing about novels and short stories is that they send out a line to the rest of the world and people catch that line and you hold that line and you're connected to everyone else.

Originally broadcast November 1, 2004.

20

Shelby Foote
Writing the Civil War

*It's ironic that one of America's greatest southern writers may be best
remembered by his speaking voice, but television will do that. Shelby
Foote, who dedicated twenty years of his life to writing one of the
greatest Civil War anthologies ever produced, as well as seven novels,
achieved celebrity status after appearing in Ken Burns's acclaimed
documentary,* The Civil War. *Giving expression to a kind of interior
southern reality that outsiders often fail to grasp or appreciate,
Foote made lasting contributions to our understanding of the South,
our American heritage, and the complex issues of victory and defeat.
Shelby Foote died on June 27, 2005.*

✻

George Seay: You've accepted the description of being a southern
writer, Shelby—what does it mean to you to be a southern
writer, given the distinct history and culture of the South?

Foote: Of course, southern writers differ greatly from each other,
but they have certain things in common. Most of us come from
middle-size towns, rather than cities, for some reason. To me, to
be southern includes that very much.

GS: I've always been struck by your emphasis on the person in
your writing.

Foote: Right. I've said this before, but I differentiate between two types of writing, one of which I consider bad and the other good. It seems to me that a bad writer says, "How about a situation in which a man does so and so?" and a good writer says, "How about a man who in a situation does so and so?" In other words, in good writing, the character comes first.

GS: I think that's relevant not only in your novels, but in your historical writing as well.

Foote: Right. Incidentally, almost anything I say about fiction applies to history. I felt very much the same writing both of them.

GS: You say there's not fact and fiction. It's all fact.

Foote: You have to put it in quotes when you make something up, but you still respect it as highly as you do a fact that comes out of documents.

GS: Before we turn to your novels, I want to turn to the young Shelby Foote. It seems to me that books have always been a big part of your life, as well as the authors Proust, Tolstoy, and William Faulkner.

Foote: Yes, and I'll give you a good example of it. There was no bookstore in Greenville, Mississippi, where I grew up. So I got the catalogs of all the publishers and used what little money I had to order books directly from the publisher. I would order a book and know that it would be there within seven or eight days, and starting on the fifth day I'd go out and sit on the curb and wait for the postman to bring my book.

I became very excited about reading. I'd read all my life. Children's versions of *Gulliver's Travels* and *Robinson Crusoe*, and of course all the books like *Tom Swift* and before that the *Bobbsey Twins*. But for a Sunday school prize, I got *David Copperfield* when I was about eleven, and I knew as soon as I was into that book that there was a world more real than the world I lived in.

I knew David better than I'd ever known myself, or anyone else, and I began to see that in the close atmosphere of a novel you find a clarity that you can't ever find in real life.

GS: Hearing you say that makes me understand why it's all fact to you. The well-written literary character is more real than a lot of others.

Foote: That's right and it applies in all kinds of ways. We were talking about O'Hara the other morning and we were talking about how his dialogue doesn't play on the stage or screen. The same thing was true of Fitzgerald. They are great writers of dialogue, but people don't talk that way. Not really. They sound marvelous off the page, but when you put them on the stage, they don't sound right. People don't talk with those rhythms. They don't talk with that logic. They don't talk with that clarity. And thank God they don't. It would be unbearable.

GS: Did you get different lessons from each of these authors?

Foote: Absolutely, and I learned a lot of things were so false. I read article after article, book after book, that said that Dostoyevsky knew nothing about form—that he just sat down and scrawled and while he's a magnificent writer, he knew nothing about form.

Dostoyevsky has a narrative drive those people never dreamed of, and it's just incredible that they can think he didn't know how to organize a novel. He did. He did indeed.

GS: Talk to me about Marcel Proust.

Foote: He hung the moon for me. He's the writer, after Shakespeare.

GS: You've made a great point about him because a lot of people will pick up Proust and they say that his work is beautifully written but very digressive. You say no.

Foote: He's after that story every minute. He's moving that story forward and it's an enormous story with so many facts.

GS: Is it correct to think that the things you learned from Proust influenced not only your novels, but also the writing of the histories?

Foote: Absolutely—Proust called attention to the extreme importance of metaphor and simile. He said that the best way to describe the thing is to tie it in with something that's totally different from it, and yet call attention to the similarities to bring out that aspect of this thing that you're describing. I did that time and time again writing the histories.

GS: I want to ask you about your method, because I know a little bit about it and I find it fascinating. Talk to me about discipline and the sort of schedule you set, and the importance of plot and outline in all that you do.

Foote: There's a rigor there all the time, but it's not to tie me up—it's to set me free. A good strong outline gives you a platform to stand on, so then you're free to do anything you want without fear of the floor falling out from under you.

It's good to go back and spend hours like nine to twelve and then two to five, whether the writing is going well or bad, and just sweat it out. That makes you work hard. It's all trickery in a sense. For instance, you develop work habits that are so strict and work so hard because you learn to feel guilty if you didn't sweat and took it easy.

GS: Would you say about five hundred words a day would be a good day?

Foote: Five hundred words is a good day to me. I've written as many as two thousand, and as few as none, but five hundred is a good day to me.

GS: You said on one occasion that writing is a religion to you.

Foote: Yes, that is a result of my not having any other religion, so writing is my religion.

GS: It's almost standard to ask a distinguished novelist: Is your writing a revelation of the wisdom you've gained, or a search for answers to questions you're concerned about?

Foote: It's entirely a search. If I knew the answer, I wouldn't be interested in the search. It's always that. T.S. Eliot put it best: He said, "We're always after something, and then when we find it, we're no longer interested in looking for it."

GS: Those are great words. How about these other great words that I've heard from D.H. Lawrence. He said that the novel, the place where this search takes place, is the one bright book of life.

Foote: I quote that to myself all the time. I believe that too. The novel may be headed toward its death—it's been said to be for the last fifty years. First, the movie was going to replace it, now the television is going to replace it, and so on.

That may be true, but I don't know of any form that gives you the freedom to say what you want to say, make the points you want to make, and get the general satisfaction of good writing. I don't know of any form that comes close to it.

The novel may yet vanish someday, but I can't imagine what would take its place. I can't imagine a screenplay. You see writing for the theater and the greatest of all writers wrote for it—Shakespeare—but it's nearly always a sort of collaboration; not only among the actors, but the director as well, and who's going to say this line, and this should be said that way, and that and the other.

In the novel, you don't have that and you don't listen to any editor or anybody else. You just do it your way if you want to be happy.

GS: That's well said, and I believe every bit of that. I love the novel. Long may it reign.

I want to turn now directly to your novels. You and William Faulkner, whom you knew and who was certainly a close friend of yours, are remarkable to me in your use of a kind of geography. The only other place I've seen this is in Latin America, where I spent a lot of time.

Foote: You take what you want of the land and make it your own and you feel very proprietary about it. In fact, when Faulkner drew a map of his county, he put down "William Faulkner: Sole owner and proprietor." He felt that way about it.

Incidentally, I found that to carry over very much into history. When you write about a place in a certain time, with certain people involved, and you do a good job of it, you acquire a belief that that belongs to you. You can go stand and look at that ground and say: that is mine. I captured it. It's a very strange feeling.

GS: Faulkner said your book *Shiloh* (Dial Pres, 1952) was the best war novel he had ever read.

Foote: That superb accolade from William Faulkner was never spoken to me. He told his stepson Malcolm that—he never told me. Someone asked him once, after he had expressed admiration for a young writer—it may have been me, I don't know—why he didn't just tell the young writer that himself. Faulkner said, "You never stop a running horse to give him sugar."

GS: Let's talk about the importance of humor.

Foote: I've said before, and I'll always say, that I don't think there's a single page of great writing that doesn't have something funny on it. It may be sardonic. It may be the juxtaposition of two words that you don't think should go together and yet do. Shakespeare is a good example of that. He's absolutely loaded with it. *Macbeth* is irony from start to finish.

GS: We talked earlier about the novel and its importance, and I think we both agree, and certainly pray, that it continues to endure. But do you have a sense that its audience is still there and as powerful as it should be?

Foote: I have a sense that it's there potentially. I, like many men when they reach my age, say there's nothing good around, and that seems to me to be profoundly true. However, that's correctable. It's always correctable. I'm sure that when various people died—Sherwood Anderson, Theodore Dreiser, God knows, Mark Twain—everybody said, "Oh, Lord, literature is finished," and there Faulkner and Hemingway and Fitzgerald were chugging along full force. I like to think that maybe they are today, although perhaps I don't see them just as those before didn't see their successors as continuous of the tradition.

GS: I began reading your three-volume history of the Civil War just after I read *Shiloh*. I think that's fortunate because it seems to me that the same things are important in both these works—character. Human character. And rigorous, I mean absolutely thorough, dedication to a factual retelling of the tale. So even though the one was a novel based upon the events and the other is a history of those events, it's the same dedication to fact.

Foote: History, after all, is an act of men and the way to understand it is to try to understand the men who made it.

That's where the interest lies. That's what makes it worth a grown man's time to look into what these people are like that did this dreadful thing or saved us from this dreadful thing. Abraham Lincoln is Abraham Lincoln, and he's so complex in his makeup as to be in the genius category. He's fascinating to study and a wonderful treat to write about.

GS: And through understanding his character we get a better sense of his motivation and the motivations of others.

Foote: Absolutely. I suppose most people would agree with me that he's our greatest president. Then you get into why he is our greatest president. One of the reasons was he had to be our greatest president to save this country. But it's more than that. Lincoln's complexity is almost infinite.

For instance, in opposition to Jefferson Davis. Davis was badly crippled by having to keep his word and preserve his honor and be a gentleman. Lincoln would break his word to you in a minute if he thought it would help save the union. Being a gentleman was no part of his calculation. And as for his honor, he was perfectly willing to let other people worry about that. He himself would want to do what was right and if that's not honorable in somebody's eyes, so be it. But he has this marvelous flexibility.

We just went through a presidential campaign where they called the winner, Clinton, shifty and slick and this and that and the other. The two shiftiest presidents I know of are the two greatest presidents—Lincoln and Franklin Roosevelt. Either one of them would give you his solemn word and break it two days later if he thought it was good for the country. I'm not equating Clinton with Lincoln and Roosevelt, but it fascinates me that he should be criticized for being shifty when these two greatest of our presidents were the shiftiest of our presidents. Lincoln was a true political genius and many other things, too.

GS: Lincoln could be mystical on the one hand, but he was pragmatic on the other.

Foote: He had a quality that I still can't explain. He could stand outside himself and study himself. That is very strange. And do it with a clear eye. He could make a judgment on himself. The only other person I knew to do this, strangely enough, is a person whose weakness of character is famous—F. Scott Fitzgerald. He could look at his work the way Lincoln could look at himself.

GS: What can you tell us about Jefferson Davis?

Foote: I used to think that Davis had an easier time than Lincoln because he didn't have an opposition party. Lincoln had to function all the time with the Democrats in mind and what they were going to do, whereas Davis didn't have two political parties. But many of Lincoln's greatest effects came from having to ride these two horses at the same time, whereas Davis didn't have this kind of balance that he had to keep. So it was not an advantage. He didn't have the spur of doing unusual things to satisfy this group of people. In fact, he made more enemies within his party than Lincoln made in the opposition party.

GS: It's delightful to find many of the same qualities in both your novels and your histories. When you describe Lincoln's train trip from Springfield to Washington to take office, I felt for the first time, though I'd read accounts of that elsewhere before, like I was on the train with him.

Foote: I'm glad, because I was truly with him. Henry James is a very great influence on me and he's the one who established how important point of view is in the novel and I try to have some point of view in the history always. I come at it from Lincoln's direction. I come at it from Davis's direction. Or Lee's or Grant's or Sherman's or Bedford Forrest's or whoever.

To me, it heightens the reality, the believability, the authenticity of the thing if you know where you're standing or looking at something.

GS: It's worth it at this point, I think, to have you comment again on a view I think you've expressed in the past. We're talking about history and we're talking about the use of detailed motivation and revelation of character and place in the context of that history. There's another genre with which this should never be confused—historical fiction, of which you do not have a very high opinion.

Foote: I have a low opinion of it, that's right.

GS: And this includes *War and Peace*.

Foote: Absolutely. *War and Peace* is a splendid example of what I'm talking about. Napoleon in *War and Peace* is a tired man on the Elbe. It's wrong to distort history. It's disrespectful to the people involved. It's not only disrespectful of Napoleon—it's disrespectful of Billy the Kid to put him in a book and not have the true Billy. Any historical character in any novel of mine is not going to say or do anything I don't know that he said and did at that time and in that place.

GS: Turning back to the Civil War, do the names of the great battles—Manassas, Shiloh, Antietam, The Wilderness—add to our sense of it as our Trojan War, our great American battle?

Foote: I think very much so. Those names take on a resonance because of what happened. After all, if you go to a field where 17,000 men, or in the case of Gettysburg, 50,000 men were casualties, that ground takes on a very real thing for you when you look at it.

And it's the reason—I take almost no part in politics or political action or anything like that—the one thing I will get out and work for is saving these battlefields. We saved Manassas from Disney a year ago. They were going to put an amusement park there. My objection was not only the destruction of the ground on which these people fought and bled, but also what I thought would be a sentimentalization of what those men did. It was going to be a theme park about the battle. Well, you can sentimentalize Mickey Mouse if you want to, but don't sentimentalize Lee and Meade and the rest of the people.

GS: You spent twenty years writing your histories of the Civil War. In the end, what did that war resolve and what did it leave unresolved?

Foote: It resolved which way this country was going and it resolved which way this country was not going. Fairly early in the war, Robert Toon gave it the best definition. He said, "I look at it as a war between two forms of society, and we're going to see which way we go."

And he was not simply talking about slavery, although he certainly included that. He was talking about other things. He was talking about an agrarian way of life, for example, in contrast to an industrial way of life. I look on it somewhat that way too. I don't regret that the South lost the war. The big compromise suits me. That is, it's probably best that the country remained one country, and I also believe that the South fought bravely for a cause in which it believed. That's the great compromise, and I got with that and I hate to see that violated.

GS: You're pretty unsparing in your narratives about the kinds of blunders—I don't know if I should go so far as to call it American stupidity—that led to bloodshed.

Foote: It was stupid. It was extraordinarily stupid. But men are stupid and they do stupid things, and sometimes they do them on a huge scale. The horrors of the twentieth century were still in the future, but they were bad enough in the nineteenth. It was a failure to do the very thing this country was founded on—they couldn't reach a compromise. Instead they had to go out and kill each other in enormous numbers. There were over a million casualties in the Civil War.

GS: Your three-volume series began when Bennett Cerf, the late renowned publisher, asked you to do a short history of the Civil War.

Foote: His plan was to start a historical series. I figured it would be very easy. It's all sitting right there in the books. So I sat down and outlined it, and I hadn't even started writing before I saw I wasn't faintly interested in writing a 200,000 word summary of what happened during the war. I didn't see that would add to anybody's knowledge of the war or anything else.

So I got really interested and organized the whole three volumes right there in a period of about two or three weeks and wrote back and said I couldn't do the short thing but I'd like to go spread eagle and do the three volumes. They'd be big. I didn't know how big then.

GS: And then it took twenty years to write.

Foote: It took me five years to do the first volume, five years to do the second volume, and then I took a break for a year. It was ten years before the third volume came out, and each of them is longer than the one before.

I had heard of a French soup that's strongly condensed and as you stir it with a spoon, it swells in the bowl. And I felt I was engaged in eating one of these huge historical soups—it kept swelling in the bowl.

GS: The past decade has brought a big popular resurgence and interest in the Civil War. The Ken Burns series, of which you were such a vital part. Novels like *The Killer Angels*. Films like *Glory*. The public interest seems to be rekindled. Do you think it's a deep enough interest, and even if it is, how important is it to sustain that interest?

Foote: It's never deep enough, but I think it's deep enough for people to have begun at least to see what a fascinating subject it is, and I think that will hang on for a good while. I certainly do think that people should understand what I call this crossroads of our being. If you're going to understand anything about modern America, you have to see where it took off from.

Ken Burns's series was even better than people realized. I was in on the birthing of it. He sent out a first draft of the narrative that's read during the program and he sent it to about twenty-four historians who knew something about the Civil War, and then when we had time to read it, he asked us to come up to Washington. About twenty of us did, and we sat around a huge table and went through this thing page by page.

There was nothing that came up that there wouldn't be at least five or six men in that circle who knew everything about it, and if there was any doubt about the authenticity of something, or any doubt about which version of something he should use, Ken was willing to accept that. In other words, he knew from the start that he couldn't attain the truth, but the closer he got to the truth, the better that program would be; so no matter how much value he placed on the drama of the scene, he was willing to drop it in a minute if he didn't think it was authentic. And that was what made us willing to work with him on it and that's what wound up making the series a good series.

Originally broadcast January 20, 1997.

21

Kathleen Norris
Revisiting Church,
Reinterpreting Language

Kathleen Norris is an award-winning poet and author.
Focusing on the spiritual life, her books are deeply personal,
full of reflection, critical yet reverent, amusing, stimulating,
and important. In her most recent work, Amazing Grace: A
Vocabulary of Faith, *Norris explores theological concepts such*
as doubt, belief, and perfection in the context of day-to-day
human experience, allowing these words to become more than
the workings of the intellect.[1]

✺

George Seay: Kathleen, tell us why you wrote *Amazing Grace.*

Norris: Well, I started going back to church a good twenty years after having walked away when I was in high school. After high school, I drifted away from church as many baby boomers in my generation did. And when I went back to church twenty years later, I felt like I was being bombarded with a number of theological words in even an ordinary Christian worship service.

---

1. Kathleen Norris, *Amazing Grace: A Vocabulary of Faith* (Riverhead, 1998).

Even the word *Christ*—people would say "the peace of Christ," and I wouldn't know what they meant by that. As a poet, I was intrigued and bothered and interested, and I just had to start investigating the words that floated around those worship services, which really was what led to this book.

I wrote the book for myself, as part of my process of beginning to come to an adult accommodation of these words. I had my childhood experiences of them, which were sometimes rather joyful, sometimes not. As an adolescent, so much of the language of the Christian faith had been so abstract to me and intellectual, and what I needed to do was to grasp a more existential sense of the words as reflecting a lived faith. Christianity is not a philosophy—it is a way of life.

GS: That brings up something I want to talk about. In this book, you don't go in the direction of therapy.

Norris: I tried not to. I am a literary person, and I'm not trying to write a self-help book. I'm also not trying to proselytize. One of the graces for myself as a writer is that my editor is Jewish, so she wouldn't let me proselytize, even if I did want to, and that's been a real gift. As with many people who have engaged in interfaith dialogue, I have found that working so closely with someone who comes from another faith tradition has forced me to articulate my own faith in a deeper way than I probably would have if I didn't have that extra pressure from her questioning what Christians mean by this or that word. "I'm a Jew; I don't understand." That alone made the writing of this book really enjoyable for me in ways that I could not have predicted for myself.

GS: That interfaith enrichment reminds me of your earlier book about the Benedictine monastery.[2]

Norris: And, of course, the Benedictines do not proselytize either. They simply are. They exist in their monasteries and welcome guests. They do what they do, and you can come and participate or not. I am much more comfortable with that approach to Christianity than reading writers or meeting people who are always trying to convert me to their version of the Christian religion.

Neither am I trying to say that I'm the expert now and this is what this word means and you should get in line behind me. I am simply reflecting on my own experience of the words which I found. Quite early on, I began to find that I had strong opinions about many of these words, but often my opinions were based on ignorance and stereotypes.

The word *belief* was one that really startled me because I think that most of the time now, when people ask you what you believe, they're really asking you what you think. It has been reduced to an intellectual concept. The word *belief*, at its root, means to give one's heart to that which is a whole other thing than merely intellectual assent. It's a much richer word than I realized, and more liable to ambiguity in that sense. If you give your heart to something, there's good and bad involved in that. It's a real commitment, and a whole relationship. It's not just an intellectual assent or an intellectual category.

Another word that was really opened up for me was a very scary word—*perfection*. There's that gospel passage: "Be perfect as your heavenly Father is perfect." I always used to find that a depressing thing to hear on Sunday morning, and then some scholar friends of mine pointed out that the word *perfect*, as

---

2. Kathleen Norris, *The Cloister Walk* (Riverhead, 1996).

used in the gospels, really reflects a word that meant more what we would mean by *mature* or *ripe, full-grown,* or *complete.* And this sense of God as being all of that—complete, full-grown, completely mature—that's what we should strive for. That makes a lot more sense to me than what we mean today by perfect, which implies a kind of perfectionism.

GS: I'm so glad you gave that example, because from childhood onward, that has always been one of my great barriers, because it seemed so far beyond me or anything I could imagine me being; so, it was daunting even to think that you could strive for that sort of traditional view of perfection as being perfect. I find this notion of it being mature, and full, and approaching God, very inviting.

Norris: I think I can retain the sense of God as whole and complete and full in ways that I can never be. No human being can be. But now, I have a way to understand that passage of "be perfect," as God asking me to simply grow up, to become ripe, to accept who I am but with this goal of trying to be more the person that God has intended me to be. That is perfectly livable, whereas that other notion of perfection is not.

GS: Another word that I'm interested in right now is the word *doubt.* Allow me to quote a perfect biblical introduction to the question: "Lord, I believe, help thou my unbelief." It seems to me you have wrestled with doubt at certain points throughout your life, and perhaps still do. What has that been like for you? Does it persist even when one comes to a higher acceptance of belief? Does doubt still persist?

Norris: You know, for so many years, when I was trying to make my way back to church, I would go to church in fits and starts, and I would be angry at something I would hear in the scriptures or in the sermon. The language would turn me off and even the minister would say that I was getting too worked up over this. He'd tell me to give it a rest for a while. Don't come to church for a while. And I really did struggle through a lot of doubt over everything connected with the Christian faith, so the word is highly significant for me.

I guess one great step I took on my journey, though, was when I was visiting a monastery for the first time, and I had thought that my doubts were rather spectacular and that they were certainly obstacles to my faith. And this one wise, gentle old monk said, "Oh, no—doubt is a sign that faith is alive. Doubt is the seed of faith." And no one in my life had ever expressed it to me that way, and I thought what a wonderful door was opening there. I can pursue my doubt and maybe it will lead to something that is not doubt.

And in fact that is definitely what has happened. I still believe that doubt is present. Emily Dickinson used to say, "I believe in a doubt a hundred times an hour which keeps believing nimble." I think, for myself now, I have a certain grounding in Christian faith. Doubts are still there, but maybe they just don't bother me as much, and they don't take center stage as much, because now that little seed of doubt has grown into something that's a little more like a tree that has roots, that I can sort of rest under, rather than go wandering off.

I used to be almost complacent in my doubts. I think that's a funny state that a lot of people get into. You get so identified with yourself as an agnostic or a doubter that you get kind of lazy. I think I did get kind of lazy and didn't pursue it any further.

GS: I found the chapter on idolatry really riveting because again, as in every case, you bring it into the meaning of daily life and explain it as something that has to do with obsession, by relating it to an ugly truth of our society—the abuse of women.

Norris: I'm glad you picked up on that. I think I originally wanted to write about idolatry because I was curious to know why the first of the commandments God gives to the Israelis is to not be idol makers and not worship idols. I began to realize that I had a very narrow and limited understanding of idolatry.

I had somehow taken the word almost too literally, and I thought, well, I'm not worshiping idols and little golden calves. I'm not even terribly acquisitive. I don't own much gold. I was thinking in these very literal terms, so that idolatry didn't seem to be my problem.

I could identify with greed and lust and some of the other sort of prime-time commandments, but I said, no, I'm not an idol maker. I thought that must have been a more primitive expression of something back then—that people worshiped graven images. It was a really false understanding of idolatry, and I began to see it in a much more complete way, as simply something people are prone to do.

I might make an idol of my first cup of coffee in the morning, if I have to shove people aside to get it. It's that question of loving yourself a whole lot more than you love anyone else and regarding anything as so important in your life. Making something so important in your life that other people sort of fall by the way. You'll do anything to get that idol. It can be a new car. It can be a higher salary. It can be a cup of coffee in the morning. It can really be almost anything.

I think human beings are incurable idol makers, and I think that the way we educate young people about love, in America at least, encourages a kind of idolatry. We encourage a very romantic view that this person you are falling in love with is everything. And what often happens is people fall in love with the idea of falling in love, but they never quite see the real person who's there and often this leads to very possessive behavior— usually on the part of men, sometimes with women—and when the real person asserts herself she's often beaten up and sometimes murdered. Because we have to keep that idol of love alive, and sometimes, in order to do that, we have to destroy the real person, because it comes into conflict with the idol. In that context, idolatry is terribly relevant in our culture.

GS: Kathleen, perhaps the most intimidating word of all is *hell*. There was something very liberating in your writing on the meaning of *hell* in your book, and you say that Christianity is not primarily a religion of hellfire and damnation. As you say, "People are judged not on what they believe, but on how they have loved."

Norris: I'm using a gospel passage there, where Jesus really says, "You will recognize me at the judgment if I've already seen you when you came to me when I was sick, when I was in prison, when I was hungry, when I was poor. We'll recognize each other." It's an incredibly intimate moment and he's really talking about the last judgment, but there is no little cute list of things. You know: if you believe this, don't believe that.

All of that is an expression of how you have loved, and that is a powerful, central gospel image for me. I think one of the things I found as I was researching this was that the image of hell exists in other religions, and so I wanted to sort of expand that a little bit because I think Christianity is so often caricatured as the religion of hellfire and damnation. You see cartoons about it. And there are denominations within Christianity that do focus on that, but there are also many that do not.

And I find it interesting that so many of the world's religions do try to figure out how God will do justice after so much injustice has been done in this world, and that's what it really comes down to. We really want to say that if someone has been oppressive and lived off of the sweat of other people and abused other people terribly, we want some notion that in the long run, they're going to pay for what they do. Maybe they never got caught in this life, but maybe they'll have to pay for it in some other form or some other fashion.

So many of the world's religions deal with that because it's sort of a universal human question. But it doesn't have to be the total focus of any religion, and I don't think it really is.

I think a really big part of what religion translates into is the requirements of daily living with other people and working with other people in this world. And as we approach the millennium, you'll see these rather hysterical millennia movements, and those are exciting. I mean, that's thrilling. You can get really carried away in all sorts of great exciting stuff, but you're still going to have to figure out a way to live every day with other people and that, to me, really is so much more important than the spectacular stuff. Worrying and wondering about what's going to happen in the future seems to me one of the most useless activities that human beings can indulge in, because we really have very little say in those matters. I always tell people when they're fretting over whether a plane is going to be on time, or over getting to the airport on time, to just think about the fact that a meteorite could come and blow us all away. Let's put this in perspective. And I think that's what we probably need to do as the millennium approaches.

Originally broadcast June 15, 1998.

22

Ann Darr
How Poetry Saved My Life

In my mind, nobody exemplifies the high qualities that Tom Brokaw assigned to the "the greatest generation" better than my favorite poet, Ann Darr. She carries herself with a joyful and supreme confidence, and I think this comes from having overcome exceptional challenges. Ann confronted many obstacles as a young woman—for wanting to serve in the military and, on top of that, to fly airplanes. During WWII, she joined the Women Airforce Service Pilots and was among the first women in U.S. history to be trained to fly military aircraft. Ann later worked as a radio personality and has published five collections of poetry.

❋

George Seay: Ann, let me start off with a question that's always fascinated me about poetry and poets, just as a way of setting a background for our conversation.

I want to use a couple of incidents from my own life. I had the pleasure, when I lived in Brazil, years and years ago of course, of knowing the poet Elizabeth Bishop. And I once asked her about poetry, and she said to me, "You know, George, it's about possibilities." And that answer really intrigued me.

And then, going back even further in my own checkered past,

when I was a student at college, we had Richard Eberhart come and talk to us. He was talking to us about poetry and what it meant to be a poet. He said it's something you surrender yourself to. Here's the phrase I remember from thirty years back. He said, "You sit in the lap of the Muses."

And from both of these experiences, Ann, I got the idea that each poet might approach this differently and have something personal to say about poetry. So I'm asking you, Ann, what does poetry, and the writing of poetry, mean to Ann Darr?

Darr: I can almost say that poetry saved my life. I grew up in a little town in the Midwest, where there was no library. And one day, when I was nine years old, I went with my girlfriend Eldred to her music lesson and her music teacher said to me, "Why don't you wait for Eldred in here," and she opened the door to her own library, which was floor-to-ceiling books. I didn't even know there were that many books in the world.

And I took one down off the shelf—*The Anthology of World Poetry*, edited by Mark Van Doren—opened it to "The Love Song of J. Alfred Prufrock," and never recovered. I didn't exactly know what it meant, but I read those words and thought that this is what the world is all about.

That dear woman let me take the book home with me, and I read and read and read, and then I wrote and wrote and wrote. It was the beginning of what has become a career, even though for years, I thought I was writing only for myself.

GS: When I think of poetry and what it's meant to me, I think of a couple of phrases. One is from Thornton Wilder's play *Our Town* where, as you probably recall, the protagonist Emily comes back to life, and as she marvels at the earth, she asks if any human beings, when they are alive, realize how wonderful life is. And the Stage Manager replies, "No," but then, after a pause, adds, "The saints and poets, maybe—they do some." It's a lovely line. A great compliment to poets, too, and probably true. And what I'm wondering, Ann, is what you think the gift of poetry is for those who read it.

Darr: It helps us understand what happens in our lives. There are those poems that one reads and you say, "Oh, yes, that's the way it is."

And you think, too, "I wish I had said that."

The poet has to be aware, has to be looking all the time, feeling all the time, and registering in some way that can then be translated into the language that we all use. Because that is how we communicate with each other. And if poems aren't the most wonderful way to communicate, I don't know what is.

GS: I was hoping you would read to us a poem you wrote called "Orders," which I think tells us a great deal about you.

Darr: I'd be delighted.

> After I ran away from home and came back again,
> my Papa said, Go if you must but mind three things:
> stay away from water, stay off of boats and don't
> go up in an aeroplane. So I first learned to swim,
> then I learned to sail, and then I learned to fly.[1]

GS: That's really where things started, isn't it?

Darr: Yes. It started really because my mother died in an automobile accident when I was three-and-a-half years old, and I had

---

1. Ann Darr, "Orders," *Flying the Zuni Mountains* (Forest Woods Media Productions, 1994), p. 55.

a childish myth that I could go to heaven and see her, and the way I would get there would be to fly under my own power.

GS: When I read your poems, I'm struck by the way you make use of human experiences in such a variety of ways—men, women, landscape, geography, time, motion, relations between mothers and daughters—all these different themes.

Darr: You mention mothers and daughters. I have three grown daughters and now also three grandchildren, I'm glad to say. But probably the poem that has been asked for most in all of my writing is one called "The Gift."

> Daughter, this small stiletto which I found
> sticking in my ribs, I have wiped clean
> and given back to you. You will need it.
>
> I had hoped there was some other way.
> Some way for you to take your self from me
> without the violence.
>
> I deluded myself, of course, until now
> I am hardly prepared for these scenes
> we play. I have forgotten,
> if I ever knew, how to repair
> my face.
>
> Can't I engage
> some Fury to play my part with me, so that
> in the climax when you leave my house
> 'forever' I can defy you, as I must if
> I would pass the prompt-book, nay the old stiletto
> which belonged to my mother's mother's mother's . . .[2]

---

2. Ann Darr, "The Gift," *St. Ann's Gut* (New York: William Morrow, 1971), p. 51.

GS: I can certainly understand why that's so popular. Masterful use of language, Ann.

I want to talk now about one of your new collections of poems, *Confessions of a Skewed Romantic,* a title I love, and I've tried to think about how I was going to ask you about that title and how you came to write it, and I thought the best thing to do would be to have you read the poem and then we'll talk about it.

Darr:

"Confessions of a Skewed Romantic"

after seeing The Butcher's Wife (a movie about a psychic)

Are we this much in need of Fairy Tale?
We are. Magic was our middle name until
our hero calmly held the mike and told us
he was HIV Positive and dread spread across
the news-type faces furrowing brows, turning down
mouths. Wasn't recession enough? Wasn't
revision enough? So small a space we kept for
heroes and one by one they drop into the well's depth,
disappear carrying our small hope handle.

Iowa didn't grow only corn. We coveted
the figures on the screen, oh Marian Davies,
swinging from the chandeliers, and Gloria Swanson
glorifying her own swan song and Clara Bow
the IT girl who knew what Marilyn
was all about before there was a doctrine
named Monroe. Oh cherished nights in
the glimmering motion room. Huddling, scrunching,
raising our breathing rate, hot cheek against
hot cheek and tender fingers, probing, pressing,
all set to music and flashing bodies on the screen.

Joe Warren ran the movie house and I ran
after his darling son and tackled him in the grass
on May Basket Day and planted enormous kisses
on his little darling face. I learned it all
in his father's movie house. Kiss him and he's yours.
The movies taught me everything I know.[3]

GS: You call this collection your movie collection of poems, don't you?

Darr: Yes, I do. I hadn't realized how much the movies had to do with my upbringing until I saw a television show recently about the Great Depression and learned that Hollywood was purposely putting out these glorious, romantic movies of musicals and comedies. Oh, how I lapped them up. They were a saving grace and they were purposely made to raise the spirits of the depressed people.

GS: And they really did so. You remind me of something else, too, Ann. You mentioned how during the Depression the movie industry made this conscious choice to put Fred Astaire, Ginger Rogers, and these glamorous people before us. People, and I must confess I'm one of them, have been a little bothered of late by how humor seems to have gone out of life in our society. People seem to be so "in your face" and confrontational. There seems to be so much anger. I wondered what you felt about that and where you place the importance of humor. You seem to give it a very high place.

Darr: I certainly do. I don't know how I could have lived my life without laughter. And what disturbs me greatly at this point in time is how humor has become so vicious. It is cutthroat. It is against the other person in ways that make me cringe. It makes

---

3. Ann Darr, "Confessions of a Skewed Romantic," *Confessions of a Skewed Romantic: Poems by Ann Darr* (The Bunny and the Crocodile Press, 1993), p. 11.

me stop my students, in fact, and say, "Wait a minute. This is not funny. This is at the expense of someone else's personality or weaknesses."

As I remember, old humor was directed against oneself, if anybody, and some of the raw jokes that seem to be in fashion at the moment go along with the violence that I abhor. I am so angry about the violence that comes more and more in television and movies. I turn these things off. I write to the people who put them together. We don't need that. We can't draw human nature as it really is without some violent streak somewhere, sometimes, but this has gone overboard to the point that it is dangerous to us as people.

GS: And this discussion of the importance of humor leads me to the next poem I was hoping you'd read for us. It's called "Claiming Aunt Edith."

Darr: This is a found poem, George; a found poem being one, in case people aren't familiar with that term, that you find someplace in writing. This poem came from an obituary. I had an Aunt Edith, but it wasn't this one. But that's the reason I have called it "Claiming Aunt Edith." Russell was my maiden name, so I felt justified.

> Edith L Russell, one of the last survivors
> of the Titanic disaster, died in a London
> Hospital Friday night at the age of 98.
>
> Miss Russell of Cincinnati, Ohio, once said
> she was saved because a sailor, finding her reluctant
> to jump into a lifeboat, snatched her lucky stuffed pig
>
> and threw it in. She could not bear to give up her pig
> and jumped in after it. It was hard to jump because
> "My dress was too tight," she said, "too tight and ankle length."

There were 711 survivors, 1513 perished, when the unsinkable
line struck an iceberg on its maiden voyage. Miss Russell
said she was the next-to-last survivor to leave the liner.

Only four are left to remember the world's greatest
peacetime disaster at sea. According to legend, the band
played on as the liner sank. "There was no music,"
she said, "just terrible screaming."

Her stuffed pig, a music box, was given her for good luck
after she survived a car crash in France. The lifeboat
was 14 stories above the water. I said, "What do you
think I am, a monkey or an acrobat." I was clutching

my pig. A sailor grabbed it and threw it into the boat,
and I said "that does it! I'm going after it" and was
able to jump. She still had the pig when she died.

People came from all over the world to touch it for good luck,
she said. The only child of a wealthy Cincinnati merchant,
Miss Russell led an adventurous life as a traveler, Paris
fashion writer and World War I correspondent. "I'm accident

prone," she said. "I've been in shipwrecks, car crashes,
fires, floods and tornadoes. I've had every disaster but
bubonic plague and a husband."[4]

GS: I can't help but laugh.

Darr: I'm glad you appreciate the humor in my poems, because
for so long I wrote from my dark side, and I tried to turn it
around and not everybody sees that my poems are funny.

---

4. Darr, "Found Poem—Claiming Aunt Edith," *Confessions*, p. 23–24.

GS: Well, I certainly see it. You call this a "found poem," and tell me if I got it right from your explanation. You find the basic information and you create the poem from that.

Darr: No. You find a poem in prose. Maxine Cumin has a wonderful poem about feeding the bears someplace in Canada, and she has taken it and stop-lined it so that it fits a poetic form, but it is exactly what the sign says. This poem is exactly what was written in the obituary that I read about Edith Russell.

GS: I want to stay with humor for a moment and ask you to read "The Terrible Secret."

Darr:

> Long before Norman Cousins
> laughed himself into good health
> and a place on a medical faculty,
> I knew what laughter could do.
>
> My verse comes from
> my dark side. I try
> my damnedest to write
> like a cross between Pablo
> Neruda and Robin Williams.
>
> It never works, of course,
> but I know what the form-
> ula is: a belly laugh.
> Not a belly dance, not a
> belly flop, but laughter
> till it hurts. I go by myself
> to hear Bill Cosby. I stayed
> up late to see Johnnie Carson. I
> don't remember the words but

I know how it feels to laugh till
my ribs ache.

And my terrible secret is
if I can't end up doubled
in laughter with my lover,
then he is no good for me.
There is no "small death" in
the climax, there is only
the belly laugh, delicious
lovers' laughter.

Do you know how I know it
is Friday? There's a pickle
in my lunch box. Significant
frog.[5]

GS: Absolutely wonderful.

Darr: You know, my papa taught me how to laugh. It's the biggest gift next to life that he gave me.

GS: There's an act of creativity that I find in just reading what you write.

Darr: Well, I appreciate that. I think that my poems are easy to move into and that's because they use a simple language; they are not complex.

It was Wilbur Schramm, the man who started the Iowa Writers' Workshop and in whose house I lived as I worked my way through college, who taught us a class that stayed together for two years in a row, if you can believe that. It was an extraordinary class, but the crux of his teaching was: Use the simple way. If

---

5. Darr, "The Terrible Secret," *Confessions,* p. 41.

there is a more simple way to do it, use that. And that stuck with me completely.

GS: Always use the simple, direct ways—like direct navigation. Just stick to her straight.

Darr: That's right. You must be a pilot.

GS: I am a pilot.

Darr: How well I could tell.

GS: Speaking of direct navigation, Ann, and flying, I want to conclude with a poem from your other collection of poems, "Flying the Zuni Mountains."

Darr: Yes, that's the name of this book.

> Hold death by the heels
> and tickle his nose with a feather,
> for the wind is our blood
> it will blow itself away.
> Never a dark red rivulet trickling through the grass
> beside the bolts and the pressed-wood props made in
> Camden, New Jersey.
>
> Let the engine drone a funeral dirge,
> the sharp staccato when one cylinder plays alone.
> The quiet , , , just the wind.
> No sound when the ribs crumple,
> like the old tree falling in the forest
> with no one to hear,
> for we are not there.
> We stand and lean on a cloud
> and call for another beer.

This we know:
we are the wind.
We will come back gently over the lake,
we will lash the waves and bend the trees;
we will lie side by side on the high mountains
drinking martinis and telling the old jokes over.
Never our wings will melt or crumple with heat or hardness.
This we know.
For the man who draws the blueprints, shapes the wings,
threads the bolts, pulls the props
is not our faith.
Ours is the wind and the wind is us
and no one shall bury us ever.

We have known space not surrounded by closets and
cabbages cooking,
we have whirled rainbows over our heads;
we have owned the earth by rising from it,
never again shall we walk with ordinary feet.

The wings were shaped from a woman's weeping . . .
no other tears shall fall.[6]

GS: Wow.

Darr: That was true. Raindrops on a window pane made the designer look at a teardrop and how it floated down a face and, the wing was designed on a teardrop.

GS: That poem is about a lot more than just flying airplanes.

Darr: Well, yes. Actually, all the poems are about more than what they actually say. I think most poetry is. Most good poetry has

---

6. Ann Darr, "Flying the Zuni Mountains," *Flying*, p. 25.

several levels and shows the depth that one can relate to only by reading it over and over.

GS: I'm glad to hear you say that. Ann. To conclude, I want to ask you about something that's been on my mind. We've established that humor is important. But talk to me about adventure, and its importance in your life. Adventure. Daring.

Darr: Yes, of course, risk. Risk is the word. A writer risks putting himself, herself on the page, by writing down what something really means. Where one lives—it's not in the head, it's in the belly. It's the emotional contacts with other people and other situations. So, I don't mean to live dangerously, particularly because I was kept from doing all kinds of things when I was little by my father, who was overly protective after my mother died in an automobile accident. He wouldn't even let me drive a car. I learned to fly before I could drive a car. One makes those leaps in poetry and one makes those leaps in life as far as one is able, and it depends on what you want and how hard it is to get it.

Originally broadcast October 24, 1994.

23

Arthur Golden
Thinking Outside the Culture

I've long believed that many of the greatest gifts of literature come from those who use the power of artistic imagination to transcend borders, and this is certainly true for Arthur Golden, author of Memoirs of a Geisha.[1] *Committing himself to a decade of disciplined, patient research, Golden managed to cut across boundaries of culture, gender, and generation in order to craft an intimate portrait and exposé of the Japanese geisha during the 1930s and 40s. The novel became a* New York Times *best-seller and was released as a major motion picture in 2005.*

※

George Seay: I guess the inevitable first question you must face in practically every conversation is how an American male of our time can so artfully project a reality that's so foreign and distant. It seems to me that you threw out the window the advice that all aspiring authors are routinely given: write what you know. It appears that you decided to write about what sparked your imagination. Am I right?

Golden: Absolutely. This is clearly a case of writing something very unfamiliar to my own background and experience. But I

---

1. Arthur Golden, *Memoirs of a Geisha* (Knopf, 1997).

tend to tell students to know what you write, so that you just have to be responsible about learning the world that you intend to write about, even if it is rather foreign.

And the most important thing, as you say, is to write what sparks your imagination. Henry James used to talk about his idea of what he called a *donee*—something that sparks your imagination, and in fact, he would interrupt people in the middle of a cocktail party who would be telling him an anecdote and he'd say, "No, no, no, I don't want to hear anymore," because he was afraid it would spoil a spark that he had been given. I think it is important never to turn away from that sense of inspiration.

In my case, I had a background in Japan, and that put me in a position to feel that I had at least a foundation to begin building on. I think if my imagination had been sparked by something completely alien to my own background and experience—Zulu culture or something—I would have had a much, much longer road ahead of me.

GS: I like that phrase—"know what you write"—because it seems to me that among the obligations of this kind of approach comes the obligation of a tremendous amount of research. Just plain, tough, disciplined searching out of facts. Is that the case?

Golden: It is the case, and it's funny, because just this past weekend, I spent the weekend with the costume designer and set designer who are beginning to work on the film, and the costume designer and I were talking about one fairly obscure piece of information concerning costumes.

I say piece of information, but we were talking about something that we didn't know. We were trying to sort out an answer. He said, "Well, you know, most people are going to shrug their shoulders and say, 'Ah, it's good enough.' There are only about ten people in the world who would know that it's wrong."

Then he made a face that made it clear to me that he didn't approve of that sort of an attitude, and I said, "You know, it's funny, but I sometimes had to tell myself that as I was writing this book. If I get it wrong in some cases, there will only be twenty-five people who know," and I stopped there and he didn't look comfortable.

But then I said, "But you know what the truth is?" And this is true—"I always did try to find the answer. It was only when I couldn't find it that I gave up and said it's good enough."

He jumped enthusiastically on that and said that was exactly his approach in designing costumes as well. You try the hardest you possibly can, and when you finally run into a stone wall, you make your very, very best guess.

GS: I think that answer should be graven in stone for everyone who aspires to write and write creatively. Just for the record, this obligation that you undertook came in the form of a ten-year project—two drafts of 800 pages. Is that right?

Golden: Actually, it was three. I wrote it twice in third person. The first time I wrote it, it was based on a lot of book learning, and I thought I knew what I was talking about. But I made a lot of what I just described as sort of educated guesses based on running into stone walls. But then I met up with a geisha and interviewed her at length.

GS: Mineko Iwasaki?

Golden: Exactly. Mineko Iwasaki. Yes, in Tokyo. This was when I learned that most of the assumptions I made, which had been based on my readings, had been wrong. Completely wrong. And so I stowed that first draft away, never to look back at it again. And in fact I never have.

I wrote it again. This time I got the facts right, but it was still in third person and still focused on the life of an adult geisha. And at the end of the whole thing—after six years of work—I came to the conclusion that the book was much drier than I ever intended it to be and decided to start all over again with a completely new approach, and that's really what resulted in the final product.

GS: In that completely new approach, you found the narrative voice that carries this tale so well.

Tell us, why did you choose a geisha, Arthur? Why is the story revolving around a geisha in Japan?

Golden: When I first met with my agent, we were having a drink and she suddenly interrupted me, looking at the hand that held the drink before me, and she asked me, "Why are your fingernails so long?" I told her that I play classical guitar, so I have long fingernails on one hand and short fingernails on the other.

She said, "Oh, well, I think you should know that my fantasy about you is that you're a closet homosexual, drag queen transvestite."

I replied, "Well, I'm sorry to disappoint you. But what gave you that idea?"

She said, "Well, you know, it's your obvious obsession with geisha."

Well, I can't tell you how many times I've encountered the assumption that I have some sort of obsession with geisha that I was working out through the form of this novel. In fact, I think the opposite is the truth. If I had an obsession at all, it was with fiction, and as I worked through several drafts of an abortive first novel, over the course of seven or eight years, I was trying to learn to write fiction. In the course of trying to learn how to write fiction I came upon this subject matter and realized that it was just too well-suited for a novel and for an exploration of Japan for me to pass it up. So it was from that inspiration that I really began the research.

GS: I want to probe you on why this subject matter is so well-suited for a novel. I was really struck by how, in this Japanese society, which is so male dominated, you have this subculture that is entirely ruled and ordered by hierarchies of women. I don't know if any of that played into what made you think this was such a wonderful focus, but give me your reaction to that.

Golden: Well, it didn't factor into my thinking consciously. I couldn't have put into words what you just said when I began this project. It wasn't until I met with this geisha in Japan that I learned exactly what you just said.

I was walking around in Gion and I remember the street corner where it suddenly struck me that all the answers to the questions that Mineko had given me, and all the things she'd shown me in Gion, and all my observations in Japan were pointing to one central fact that I had completely overlooked: this was a culture completely ruled and dominated by women, and in fact, even in the years I've spent since that realization, I've never come upon any other subculture in Japan of which that can be said.

That does lend, for me at least, a tremendous fascination and makes it an interesting and perhaps somewhat peculiar look at Japanese culture. You might say it's a look at Japanese culture from the other side, because what you've said about male domination is absolutely true.

GS: Can you clarify for us exactly what a geisha is, Arthur? How would you define one?

Golden: A geisha is something that doesn't exist in any other culture that I'm aware of, and it's fairly simple to understand why, if you just keep in mind the fact that, for example, in western cultures, men and women socialize together freely and always have.

But in Japanese culture, that has never really been true. Men go out together, and women stay home and take care of the children. Like it or not, that's the way it's always been. And when men go out, to keep from being just a bunch of bleary-eyed drunks staring across the table at each other, men often hire women to sit with them and entertain them by telling jokes and flattering them and making them feel charming. They sing songs and tell stories and those kinds of things.

Those women who keep men company in the evening and, in this respect it is very chaste, are available at all levels of society. Businessmen hire bar hostesses and so on.

And that is what geisha do at the very highest level, because they are the most expensive version of this. The *gei* of *geisha* means "arts," and geisha are trained in traditional arts such as dance and shamisan, which is really like a Japanese folk instrument, like the guitar. So geisha are originally popular entertainers.

GS: Arthur, is this still possible in Japan? The book is set in the thirties and forties at a time, as I understand it, when there were 800 registered geisha in the Gion district. Does it still go on in quite the same way?

Golden: It does, in far fewer numbers. There are perhaps now only 60 to 80 geisha where there once were 600 to 800. But the experience of going to a tea house and being entertained by a geisha now is probably more similar than not to the experience in the thirties.

What is radically different is the experience of being a geisha. How geisha live, and the circumstances in which they find themselves in life, and the options that they have before them are very different because, in the thirties and forties, geisha usually became geisha through some sort of misery, either because they were sold by their parents through dire economic circumstances, or perhaps a more mature woman might find herself down on her luck and end up as a kind of geisha who never really had the proper training and isn't going to rise very far and will probably lead a very difficult life.

Nowadays, geisha are high school–educated. They enter the profession at seventeen or eighteen because it seems like fun to entertain glamorous men and they do not face the mountain of debts that a seventeen-year-old counterpart in the thirties and forties would have—the debts being the cost of purchasing her meals, her lessons, her medical expenses, and everything throughout her childhood.

GS: Arthur, in my mind this geisha subculture is one that's very much charged with erotic tension. At least I felt that in many of the exquisite passages of the book. Do you, as an author, feel some degree of caution that you would give to me or any other reader about how much we can read into the larger Japanese society from this? How should we use this as a lens to try to get some sense of what Japanese culture is all about?

Golden: That's a very interesting question. I think that, in some ways, I would have to answer both sides, yes. Yes, some caution is required, and no, some caution isn't required.

Here's what I mean. I think that subcultures very often show a kind of hypertrophy of the larger culture—a sort of over-developed quality—and I think that's certainly true of geisha society. It shows in relief, in a magnified sort of way, the hierarchical nature of Japanese society. People who are Japanese will recognize very readily the seniority system, and the method of training, and all these other kinds of things, even though they may not know the individual details.

On the other hand, it is also true that only one aspect of Japanese society is represented. The Japanese have a kind of situational ethics, we might call it. For example, in our culture, when a businessman goes out for the course of the evening, if he's seen emerging from a bar staggering drunk on the arm of a prostitute, he's going to be called onto the carpet the next morning. His fundamental character will be questioned, and he may even lose his job over it.

In Japan, that isn't traditionally true at all. In Japan, a man who goes out for the evening is out for the evening. The out-for-the-evening rules apply. A man in the office is at the office and the office rules apply, and the two things don't meet, so it's possible for a man traditionally to be a very dutiful husband and also go out and have a fling with a prostitute and all these other things, without necessarily any conflict arising. This is what I mean when I say that it represents only one aspect of Japanese society.

GS: In many of the reviews I've read, there are references to Charles Dickens and Jane Austen in the style, if not the substance, of what you've written. Are you comfortable with that? Are they influences, conscious or subconscious, in what you've done?

Golden: Yes, I think they are influences. I think Dickens shows such an interesting portrait of a world that doesn't exist anymore, and so does Jane Austen. Those are the things I think people may have in mind when they talk about similarity with my book, but there's one other issue, and that is the linearity of the book.

The book tells a somewhat traditional story in a somewhat traditional fashion, and I guess I'd have to say that I'm somewhat of a traditionalist. It seems to me that there are many arguments in favor of starting where the story begins and ending where the story ends. I think that the trendy, it seems to me, fashion of chopping up the story and giving a little piece of it here and a little piece of it there, and a flashback here, and a narrator there—that comes at a cost.

GS: Give us one argument in favor of linearity.

Golden: Well, suppose you have a fellow at a dinner party and he looks up to see that the host of the dinner party is looking at him just a moment longer than he should before looking away. Well, this is a meaningless event by itself, is quickly forgotten, and doesn't belong in a novel. But if you put a story behind it—suppose that the guest is having an affair with the wife of the host. Now, when the host looks at him a moment longer than he should, it is a bone-chilling event. It most certainly does belong in fiction.

It's the sort of thing that could alter the course of an entire life, really. You could imagine the frantic phone call in the middle of the night. "I think he knows!"

This is what a story gives. As I say, story lends momentum and meaning to events. An event means something precisely because of the context in which it occurs. I think that by chopping up stories and moving from one sensibility to another, so much of that sort of thing is lost.

That doesn't mean that there aren't times when a different approach is ideal. The example that I love to use is *The Remains of the Day.* That is, I think, just a brilliant book and what Kazuo Ishiguro achieves in that book is something much more than what would be achieved by telling the story in a linear fashion. So I don't want to say that one must always tell the story from beginning to end, but I think you have to have a good reason not to do it that way.

GS: I think the magic of projecting such an authentic character is part of what makes this such a great book. Without probing for trade secrets, I want to ask you how you manage to do that. There is one example—just to sort of key your answer—where you actually applied the makeup of a geisha as a way of getting a sense of what geishas go through in preparing for the art form they carry out. But there must be much more to it than that, as well.

Golden: I was stopped in the grocery store not long ago by somebody who said, "Now, I understand that you put on makeup and had your hair done and put on a kimono." That's not at all true. I went into the bathroom and put a tiny bit of makeup on one corner of my chin so as to have the experience of feeling it once it had dried there. That was necessary because I had to write about what it felt like.

And it is true that that sort of focus on minutiae is very much integral to creating a character. If one knows what it really is like in the world to put on makeup, you can translate that onto the page.

I think creating a character is almost like a labor negotiation, and here's what I mean. In a labor negotiation, the union says we want ten and management says we want five and you end up with something like seven and a half. Well, when you sit down and write a character out, you find your way over the course of a couple of hours to a paragraph that feels like it represents a kind of person you have in mind. The next day when you come back to read it over, you realize that it's flat, not engaging, or not interesting enough. The reader is going to work to figure out what you mean.

It doesn't come to life, so now you go back and you sort of spice it up. You make it much more vivid. And then the next day when you come and sit down to read it, you discover that it sure is vivid, but it's not the person you had in mind at all. And finally you come up with a kind of compromise which contains an element of surprise. There are all sorts of qualities that are suggested by this character that you didn't really know were going to be there.

So this is what novelists mean when they so often say things like, "Well, the character refused to do what I asked, and wouldn't marry this guy, and went off and did something else," or those kinds of answers. I think it's a really shorthand way of saying that as you begin to create the character, you find that you can't always know in advance how things are going to turn out.

GS: I was also really struck by the colloquialisms or the expressions of thought that characters regularly used in the book. They seemed so authentic. I remember there's one character whose mind is described at one point as being like a street with overloaded traffic.

Golden: Like an intersection with too much traffic.

GS: Exactly. Where do you come up with that stuff? Is that from your experience of Japan, or is that Arthur Golden's imagination?

Golden: I decided that it was essential to this character that she have an unusual way of expressing herself and there were specific reasons why I wanted that to be the case. I was struggling throughout the book to find unusual ways for her to see the world and I would get to a part where it was time for me to come up with one of these sayings that she might offer to the reader, and I would have to just see what came to mind.

I'd sit and think, "Well, she's Japanese, she's going to associate certain kinds of things. Obviously, she's not going to say anything about a computer keyboard, but what might she say?" And so in the beginning of the book, most especially the images are of water and things like frogs and fish.

After she's been in the city for a while, she then has that realm to associate to and that might include things like an intersection with too much traffic in it. It would be an inappropriate image on the first two or three pages of the book, because we haven't really seen her in the city yet, but by the time she's been there for a while, this is now part of her vocabulary. So in that way, I found myself restricted by the possibilities.

GS: Let me ask you one more question, Arthur. If not specific projects, what kinds of curiosities are now in the mind and imagination of Arthur Golden?

Golden: For one thing, I know that I'm done with Japan. I won't say that I'll never, ever go back there, but I certainly don't intend to write about that anytime in the near future, having spent so much time on it already. I'd like to find something a little closer to home. And I'm finding that one of the things that has interested me about this book was the sense of disparity between what is within and what is without. The geisha who must put on her makeup and hide away her true self and present only one aspect of that to the world—that's something that I can well imagine developing in slightly different thematic ways in my next novel, and I am sort of working now to find the material that will enable me to craft that kind of a story.

Originally broadcast October 12, 1998.

24

Norman Corwin

A Conversation with
Radio's Poet Laureate

*Norman Corwin's elegant prose has consistently captured the spirit
of the times, confronting audiences with difficult, important
questions, and his voice is still familiar to many of us. His greatest
prominence was in radio drama and journalism during the golden
age of the 1930s and 40s, most notably the weekly series of plays,
26 by Corwin, and the 150th anniversary celebration of the Bill
of Rights,* We Hold These Truths. *Corwin also wrote screenplays,
stage plays, and poetry, and even directed a few stage plays; in
2007 at the age of 97 he is still writing and teaching at the
University of Southern California.*

✳

George Seay: Where does the love of the word begin in the life of
Norman Corwin?

Corwin: It began quite early, when I did not even understand the
meaning of the word. This was before radio, television, and all
the distractions that children face today. I wandered by myself
into a branch library of the Boston Public Library system and
was boggled by the display of books around me.

I took books off shelves and I was astonished and delighted
to find that so many of them were illustrated, and one could

borrow them, and I took those home with me. Before I even understood what I was reading, I became aware of the richness of what these had to offer. And then as I grew a little older and began to put vocabulary together with meaning, I found myself very much attracted to the poets, like Keats and Shelley. I must have been about ten years old, or eleven, when I read *Endymion*, of all things. Keats is full of mythical allusions, classical allusions. But the *music* of what I was reading!

GS: I'm delighted to hear you use that word *music* because your own writing to me is symphonic in its composition, and I get the sense that Norman Corwin from a very early age sensed the rhythm of words, the cadences. Was in fact music, as apart from literature, also an influence in your work? It just drives the rhythms of your prose so strongly.

Corwin: Yes, and it continues to be. I am a failed musician and a failed composer. I had aspirations to be both. These were not to be realized because I chose the wrong instrument and found myself remarkably inept at it.

GS: What instrument was that?

Corwin: It was the violin, and my education as a musician ended when an older brother took me to Symphony Hall in Boston and I heard a performance by a genuine violinist. I found myself drawn to great music at a very early age.

GS: I'm wondering about religious curiosity as well, because in your works—particularly in the odes and the prayers—there's certainly the sense of a higher meaning in those works. Was religion a big influence on you?

Corwin: Not in any formal sense. I did extract a lot from religions that I became acquainted with through reading, and I was drawn, and am still drawn, to the ethical core of religion. I find that there is a common respect and reverence for ethics that goes through almost all of the coded religions.

GS: When I think of your works, which exemplified the golden age of radio, and these influences you and I are talking about now—classical literature, music, religious philosophy—it strikes me that your audience must have shared some of these same tastes. I'm trying to get a sense of the kinds of people, the millions of them, who were responding to Norman Corwin's broadcasts. Do you have that feeling now, looking back at that time, that people were more attuned to those kinds of values—reading more and thinking more about these things than perhaps they do today?

Corwin: Very much so. Indeed, I sometimes did programs for which the mail response, in many cases, was, I thought, better written than the programs.

GS: So there was a love of the spoken word throughout our society.

Corwin: Yes, and the heartening thing is that there are many people out there who respond to this, who are aware of it, and who want it. And, indeed, in the recent work that I've done under the parasol of Mary Beth Kirschner Productions, I have been pleasantly surprised by the response to programs of that kind. I had anticipated that the program written to commemorate the fiftieth anniversary of the bombing of Pearl Harbor

would produce limited response, but the actual response was about twenty times greater than what I had anticipated.

GS: That's so gratifying. There's still that audience out there to be reached.

Corwin: Yes, indeed. Don't let me go on, because I can turn loose on this—the obligation, I feel, of any great medium not only to serve the public interest and necessity, but to reach and give the audience more than it thinks it wants to know.

GS: What I've also found in the prose of Norman Corwin are these magnificent juxtapositions between colloquial speech and classical speech. For example, *Take a Bow, Little Guy.* Did that come from your experience working in the pre-radio days for a newspaper?

Corwin: I think it was informed by the newspaper experience, but also the influence on me of certain writers. Carl Sandburg has that quality. He is very basic, and he uses slang. He uses the idiom. Sometimes sectional idiom where we get the phrases that are current in Georgia or Montana, and the vigor of that language. Of course, this goes back to Shakespeare. He was writing in the idiom of his day, with great polish and dignity, but still there is in Shakespeare much of what we speak today in common parlance.

GS: I'm glad you mentioned Carl Sandburg, because he, of course, thought the world of the work of Norman Corwin.

But I want to turn now to another of the great qualities of your writing—the use of humor. I don't think we give humor enough importance sometimes, because many great humorists have told me that it's one way of expressing wisdom and making people aware of things that are ultimately very, very important to us. Has that been your spirit of it?

Corwin: I'm very happy to hear you say that because I feel that humor has been neglected and underrated. For example, there is one great compendium of literature that takes up several inches on my shelf and lists worldwide figures of literature, from Burma, Indonesia, Europe, Asia—throughout the world. It includes writers who are so obscure and so distant from our ken and potential interest that they can almost be discarded along with the 1961 Manhattan telephone directory. Nowhere in it did I find S.J. Perelman. Nowhere in it did I find George Aide or any of the early American humorists because they were writing humor, which was considered many rungs below tragedy.

GS: You've lamented the lack of what you call "phrasemakers" in our time, and the paucity of the language that is spoken, indicating a certain paucity of thought. I'm beginning to think, listening to you now, perhaps it's because when we underestimate things like humor, we lose grace in the process. We lose a certain graciousness, perhaps, in the way we think. In other words, there's more than a loss of listings in a compendium. There's a loss to our thought and our speech and our behavior.

Corwin: Yes, and we have only to look at the pages of the master— Shakespeare, of course—to realize the extent to which humor was useful and was one of the important colors on the pallet. I think that humor has migrated, in a sense, to graphic. We have the most trenchant humor today, to be found in the cartoons of Tony Auth, Paul Conrad, and Herblock, and that's a pity. For a while, we had satirists of the stripe of Mort Sahl, and yet there has been missing from the body of literature the kind of humor that we inherited from Mark Twain and writers of that stripe.

GS: And that is a great loss indeed. Moving into the career of Norman Corwin in radio, I want to go back to the origins. I have in mind a conversation I had with a dear friend of mine, Eric Barnouw, some years ago. Eric spoke of "the discovery of a new world, of vast new possibilities," as he went into radio. Did you have that same sense of a broad canvas upon which to paint?

Corwin: That really informed my whole outlook. I was so enthralled by the ingenuity of a species that could utilize this existing phenomenon of ether by which we can communicate across the world in the same time that it takes what I'm saying to reach your ears three feet away. I found that, to me, the opportunity to write for radio, to write for a great unseen audience, was a privilege and a gift, and I was deliriously happy to be invited to use the instruments and the technology of a medium that could accomplish this, and I'm still thrilled by it.

GS: It comes through in your works then, and just listening to you—you were extraordinarily prolific—it seems to me the medium met the man. This was the place where all these influences we've been talking about became the pallet. The colors you could use in painting these great portraits for people unseen. It amazes me how prolific you were. A play every week. How did you find that kind of inspiration and energy?

Corwin: It was monastic. I went to no movies. I went to no plays. I think I saw my girl once every three weeks. I literally retired to a thatched-roof house in the Palisades in order to be able to work concentratedly on this thing. There were couriers who would take pages from me and bring them into the city. I was not then married and engaged a cook to come by day to take care of my meals, and the rest of the time was spent writing.

GS: Perhaps one of the most striking things about a man who produces a play a week, in this era in which everyone has writer's block and is sort of proud of it, is the ability to write these things that turn from humor to high seriousness, and back and forth. Where does the inspiration for that come from?

Corwin: I think it's all around us. I think writer's block in a situation of that kind can be overcome by picking up a newspaper. Or by going to a museum. Or by listening to some music. That's where I went for my inspiration. It is not that I had command at all times, and I did have sterile periods, but I could not afford the luxury of a lengthy sterile period.

Let me back up and say that I used up my lead time of two weeks very quickly, and then, when I would leave the studio, I had no idea of what the subject of the next program would be, and I got to work on it the following morning. If it didn't come by Tuesday—my program was on Sundays—I had to abandon that and go to something else. The wonder of it is that I didn't fall flat on my face.

GS: You were also surrounded by lots of other geniuses—John Houseman, Orson Welles. The people you were involved with were absolutely fascinating. It's hard to even know how to phrase a question on this, but: Was that atmosphere as vital as I tend to believe it must have been?

Corwin: It was not to me, in the sense that I was so preoccupied with my own problem of writing, directing, and producing these programs weekly, so I had no opportunity to hear the work of my contemporaries. I think that, however, the thrust of your question is justified by the fact that there was this rich atmosphere, this rich kind of abundance of talent—Houseman, Welles, and company. That was because the gatekeepers, the program managers, were very wise in the circumstances they provided for these people.

GS: You mean the greatest amount of freedom.

Corwin: The freedom. Exactly. For example, when CBS made me the offer to be the proprietor of the Comedy Workshop for twenty-six weeks, they never said, "Give us a schematic. Tell us what these subjects will be and what the budget will be." When they asked me to do a program to commemorate the end of the war in Europe, they didn't say, "Give us an outline of what you're going to do. Let's see the first twenty pages." Nothing of that kind. They turned it over to me.

Even the hierarchy of the network—they heard the program when it was on the air. They had no previous knowledge of it.

GS: That's extraordinary. I mean, it's unbelievable in our times.

Corwin: Absolutely. Five years later, it couldn't have happened.

GS: I want to turn to some of your specific broadcasts and, if you don't mind, some of my personal reactions to having listened to them. Let me start with one called *They Fly Through the Air*. It's a piece you wrote about Mussolini's air force at the time they bombed Ethiopia. Even listening to that now, in 1996, it still gives me goose bumps, and the reason is you took exception to one description from a bomber pilot about what he called the "beauty" of what he had done. Did you feel the rage that seems to come to the voice of your narrator as you wrote that?

Corwin: I'm still enraged. I'm still enraged at the concept of anyone finding beauty in the demolition and destruction of human life, or even property. Blowing out a building. It's bad enough to have to do this to meet the demands of war, which is an ugly occupation. But to brag about it and to speak as Vittorio Mussolini, the son of Benito Mussolini, did when he dropped bombs on a group of cavalrymen is totally obscene. His description of the view from on high was that it looked like a budding rose unfolding as it blew up, eviscerating and tearing apart blood and guts of men and horses.

GS: Turning now to *We Hold These Truths*, which you wrote at the time of the 150th anniversary of our Bill of Rights. That 1941 broadcast reached and affected 60 million people. I'm fascinated by the fact that you thought it was a failure immediately thereafter. You didn't think it got the audience it did.

Corwin: That's right. You see, to me, every flaw is magnified, and as the program went along, I kept counting the flaws, not the points scored, and at the end I was sure that the accumulation of flaws had consolidated in total silence in the control room, where I had expected I might get some calls.

GS: You must be your own toughest critic.

Corwin: I think I have that distinction, yes.

GS: Let me turn now to your masterpiece, *On a Note of Triumph*. Let's talk about that because there's a part that, and I don't think I'm overdoing this at all, is a part of American history now. You commemorated our victory in Europe, but at a time when the war was not over. It's pretty complex writing, because it's not just a celebration. How did you want to approach that at a time when tragic things were still taking place?

Corwin: Part of that was a process of elimination. I had already written a good deal about war on radio, including the series that I wrote and broadcast from London during the war about our ally facing this monster. I was aware that I had to deal with an epochal, history-making, unforgettable event—the surrender of the fiercest adversary we had ever faced—and I knew that the war would not be over. They could not possibly be dancing down this street in jubilation because men's lives, the lives of fathers and brothers and sons, were at stake and there would be more killing to be done.

And that had to be recognized. And I searched, as I do with all my pieces, for structure—for something to serve as the spine of this piece. And part of the answer came from turning to my old friends Sandburg and Whitman, Shakespeare and the Bible. I found in Whitman a line that set me off and it was a line that he wrote at the conclusion of the Civil War. The line was a very simple one: "Never were such sharp questions ask'd as this day." And I thought yes, we have sharp questions to ask this day at the end of the worst war that man has ever endured.

GS: That answer makes a lot of sense, because this piece is not simply a celebratory ode. There are questions posed within it to the American people. You wanted them to be reflective of what had gone on, and what might yet go on.

It seems to me that when you do something like that you're telling us something, then and now, that democracy in its protection requires vigilance and constant self-examination.

Corwin: You're positively right. You touched on the mainspring of that piece and indeed of our ethos and national existence. There is a line in there about the importance of remembering that a muscle, to be strong, has to be used, and a faithful clock has to be wound, or given some source of energy. The same goes for anything precious in our lives, and there is nothing more precious than liberty.

GS: Let's talk about America and American society, then. Let me begin with your book, *Trivializing America* (Lyle Stuart, 1983), which first appeared in the early eighties. You were criticizing what you saw as a very affluent society that was falling into patterns of silliness. Does that indictment still hold today?

Corwin: I think it not only still holds, but it has deepened. With the proliferation of a kind of nervousness about the attention span, whereby if you watch a commercial, any commercial, the average length of any one image is a second-and-a-half to two seconds. It's a soundbite society.

Cut, cut, cut, cut, cut. Confidence in the capacity of the viewer or listener is completely abandoned.

GS: What drives that, and what's the cost of that? What do we lose by being in that state of affairs?

Corwin: We lose the benefit, indeed, the joy, of contemplation; the joy of the moment of silence. Silence, by the way, has great uses apart from healing our soothed nerves. When you think of the music of the great masters, particularly Mozart and Haydn, you'll find in the middle of their works that suddenly there's a silence; the orchestra is tacit and quiet and the music resumes so that silence becomes part of the score. It is an instrument—a muted instrument, to be sure—but it's an instrument in the orchestra.

GS: I want to ask you next about freedom of speech, which has been so important to you throughout your life. You said something that really struck me concerning free speech issues and, in particular, political correctness. "To silence an idea because it might offend a minority doesn't protect that minority; it deprives it of the tool it needs most—the right to talk back."

Corwin: I don't know that I wrote those words, but I shall read them with great interest and maybe use them again. I think that the holiest language in our national life is the language of the first amendment.

GS: One reason those words struck me so much was that you paid the price at times when people didn't want to honor free speech. I'm referring now to the McCarthy era and to "gray listing." Would you tell us about that?

Corwin: That was one of the most disgraceful periods in our entire history, and it is an example of what we were discussing earlier, of the importance of vigilance and of keeping a healthy outlook. When we lose that and get careless, or get swept along by the fulminations of some demagogue, the tendency is to relax and go with the stream, not to bother to think, not to stand out, especially if there is a penalty attached. And there were very few people in that period who stood up for the right of free speech or the right of free association.

GS: Tell us what that's like for the artist and for the society, when a person finds his or her works held up to proscription, because there's some suspicion of unorthodoxy in a political sense.

Corwin: It's debasing. It encourages in the victim an apprehension, a sense of public degradation—unmerited, but nevertheless real and vicious. There develops an awareness that old friends don't call anymore, that they somehow don't catch sight of you when you pass them on the street. The sense of being a pariah is extremely uncomfortable. When one has children, its effect spreads to the family. It has broken up families. There were victims of that black list who committed suicide. Nobody would engage them or hire them. There were people who were forced to write pseudonymously.

GS: In this season of high politics and decision making, I'm wondering about your thoughts on the political responsibility of broadcasting to our society. Specifically, what is it? Is it being met? Has it been abandoned?

Corwin: I think that it has been largely abandoned, unfortunately. In those areas of the greatest concentration of power, there are islands and archipelagoes of excellence and of responsibility, expressed in appreciation of our history, of our traditions, of the sanctity of our liberties, of all the moral furniture of our minds and our society.

That now becomes the province that represents the high

ground, where the lowlands have been flooded. And it's very important in this particular time of our lives that the harassment of our artistic programs and of the subsidization of the humanities and the arts be wheeled down. Instead, they must be built up and encouraged. The glory of ancient Greece, the Herculean Greece we so admire today, was not based on commercials. I think that what endures and what is satisfying and enriching is not only an awareness of, but the exercise of, humane instinct and the impulse to accept and to understand and to reach—not only to reach higher, but to reach a question of high purpose, transcending high profits.

Originally broadcast January 6, 1997.

List of *dialogue* Staff
1988–2007

❋

Anthony Barber
Andrea Bertone
Kirsten Dabelko
Karen Dale
Rachel Edmonds
Paul Grachow
Shaarona Harris
Kristen Hunter

Keilah Jackson
Denis Saulnier
George Liston Seay
Mary Olive Smith
Michael Switalski
John Tyler
Steven Watson